JUST SOME THOUGHTS

STEVEN ROSE

Dedicated to

My mom Norma Jean Brack. Whom I love so much.
My brother Don Rose. The smartest most talented guy I know.
My sister in law Becca who is the sister I never had.
My niece Andie and my nephew Orion. I love you guys.
My brothers and sister's at Mountain Vista Baptist church.

Contents

Chapter 1:
Invisible Man: The Unheard Voice

The moment Thomas Bradford entered a room, nothing happened. No heads turned, no conversations paused, no acknowledgment of his presence registered on anyone's face. At sixty-seven years of age, Thomas had grown accustomed to this peculiar phenomenon—his lifelong companion that he had come to call his "invisibility."

He wasn't literally invisible, of course. Standing five-foot-nine with thinning gray hair that had once been a nondescript brown, Thomas had the kind of face that photographers would describe as "perfectly average." His features weren't memorable enough to recall after meeting him, nor distinctive enough to pick out of a crowd. He dressed in muted colors—beiges, grays, and navy blues—clothes that seemed designed to blend into any background.

Thomas first noticed his condition in elementary school. During show-and-tell, other children would listen with rapt attention to Jimmy Parsons's stories about his family's vacation to Disneyland or Sarah Miller's detailed description of her new puppy. But when Thomas's turn came to share his rock collection—specimens he had carefully labeled and researched—eyes would wander, whispers would start, and his teacher would inevitably cut him short with a hurried "Thank you, Thomas" before moving on to the next child.

At first, he thought perhaps his presentations weren't interesting enough, so he worked harder on them. He practiced at home in front of his bathroom mirror, timing himself, adding animated gestures and voice inflections. Nothing changed. The same invisible curtain descended between him and his audience every time.

As Thomas navigated through high school and then college, the pattern continued with disheartening predictability. He would join a conversation among classmates, carefully waiting for a natural pause before offering his thoughts, only to find someone else talking over him as if he hadn't spoken at all. Or worse, the person he was speaking with would suddenly spot someone across the room and walk away mid-sentence, leaving Thomas with words hanging in the empty air.

"It's the strangest thing," Thomas murmured to his dog, Edison, a twelve-year-old golden retriever who was now snoring softly on his worn leather ottoman. "At least you listen to me, old boy."

Thomas's small ranch house in Millfield was comfortable if modest—a lifetime of working as an accountant had provided him with financial stability, if not wealth. The walls of his study were lined with bookshelves, each one filled to capacity with volumes on history, theology, astronomy, and classical literature. Knowledge had been his solace, his constant companion when human connections proved elusive.

Tonight, as on most evenings, Thomas sat in his favorite armchair, reading glasses perched on the end of his nose, a cup of chamomile tea cooling on the side table. The blank document on his laptop screen glowed accusingly back at him. He had been trying to start a new story—one about the woman at the well from the Gospel of John—but the words wouldn't come.

Instead, his mind kept returning to what had happened earlier that day at the church potluck. He had been explaining to Deacon Reynolds about a fascinating book he'd just finished on archaeological evidence of biblical events when Martha Simmons had approached.

"Jim!" she had exclaimed, addressing the deacon as if Thomas had suddenly vanished. "I need your help with the youth group planning committee. Do you have a minute?"

And just like that, Deacon Reynolds had turned away, completely forgetting that he had been in the middle of a conversation with Thomas. Not even an "Excuse me" or "I'll catch up with you later." Just... nothing.

Thomas had stood there, fork suspended midway to his mouth, watching them walk away. After sixty-four years, it still stung every time.

"Maybe I really am invisible," he whispered to Edison, who opened one eye briefly before returning to his dreams of squirrel chases. "Maybe that's my superpower, except I never figured out how to turn it off."

Thomas sighed and set his laptop aside. He walked to the bookshelf and ran his fingers along the spines of his biblical commentary collection. These books had never interrupted him or walked away. They had been patient teachers, revealing their wisdom at his pace, never making him feel insignificant.

His social invisibility had taken its toll on his romantic life as well. There had been women he'd admired from afar—like Sarah Jenkins from accounting who shared his love of classic films, or

Rebecca from his church's Bible study with her kind eyes and thoughtful questions. But whenever he worked up the courage to engage in conversation beyond pleasantries, the same pattern emerged. Their eyes would drift, they would find reasons to end the conversation, or—most painful of all—they would simply not notice when he approached them again at the next encounter.

In his twenties, Thomas had blamed his shyness. In his thirties, he'd tried to reinvent himself—joining public speaking classes, reading books on charisma, even briefly seeing a therapist who suggested he might be projecting his insecurities onto others. By his forties, resignation had begun to set in, though he still occasionally harbored hope for connection. Now, in his sixties, he had largely accepted solitude as his lot in life.

"Perhaps that's why I can hear God more clearly," Thomas reflected, speaking to the empty room. "With less human noise, I can focus on the divine."

His faith had been his cornerstone through all the loneliness. Thomas had been raised in the southern Baptist church, and while he had explored other denominations in his adult years, he had always maintained a personal relationship with God that felt more real than many of his human interactions.

Thomas returned to his chair and picked up his Bible, worn from years of study, its margins filled with his neat handwriting. He had always found solace in the stories of those who felt overlooked— Hagar in the wilderness, the widow with her mite, the lepers Jesus had healed when everyone else had cast them aside.

"They were seen," Thomas whispered. "Really seen."

A thought struck him then—perhaps his invisibility wasn't a curse but a calling. Perhaps God had given him this peculiar cross to bear so that he might understand the experience of the overlooked and forgotten in Scripture. And perhaps, through his writing, he could give voice to those biblical characters who had been relegated to the margins of the greater narrative.

Thomas adjusted his glasses and pulled his laptop back onto his knees. With renewed purpose, his fingers began to dance across the keyboard:

"The sun beat down mercilessly on the limestone path to Jacob's well. The woman adjusted her water jar on her shoulder, feeling its weight less than the burden of shame that had forced her to come at noon, when no one else would be there. She had become accustomed to being invisible—it was safer that way—until a stranger asked her for a drink and, for the first time in years, truly saw her..."

The words flowed more easily now. Thomas wrote well into the night, stopping only when Edison nudged his leg, asking for his nightly backyard visit. As Thomas stood watching his aging companion sniff around the perimeter of the small yard, stars twinkling overhead in the clear night sky, he felt a peculiar peace settle over him.

"Maybe this is it, Edison," he said as the dog ambled back to the porch. "Maybe I've spent all these years feeling invisible so I could write about the invisible ones in the greatest story ever told."

Thomas's attempts at career success had always faltered. He had tried starting a small tax preparation business in his thirties, but clients never returned for a second year. He had written educational pamphlets for his church that were politely accepted and promptly forgotten. He had volunteered to teach Sunday School, only to find the children as inattentive as his classmates had been decades earlier.

But writing—writing was different. On the page, Thomas's voice could not be interrupted. His stories could not be walked away from mid-sentence. The characters he breathed life into would exist as long as someone turned the pages.

Back inside, Thomas saved his work and closed his laptop. As he prepared for bed, completing his nightly ritual of brushing teeth, taking his blood pressure medication, and setting out clothes for the morning, he felt something he hadn't experienced in years: anticipation.

"Tomorrow," he told his reflection in the bathroom mirror, "we'll write about Zacchaeus—another invisible man until Jesus called his name."

Thomas climbed into bed, Edison settling into his customary spot at the foot. As sleep began to claim him, Thomas offered up a prayer of gratitude.

"Lord," he whispered into the darkness, "I've been asking the wrong question all these years. I kept asking why you made me invisible when I should have been asking what you wanted me to see because of it. Thank you for your patience with me. Please guide my hands and heart as I write these stories. Let me be a voice for those who, like me, have felt unseen. And if it's your will that these stories reach others, I trust you to make that happen. Amen."

Outside his window, a shooting star traced a brilliant path across the night sky—seen by no one but carrying on its celestial journey nonetheless. Thomas Bradford drifted into sleep, dreaming of well women and tax collectors, of shepherds and servants, of all the seemingly ordinary people through whom God had done extraordinary things.

In the quiet darkness of his bedroom, the invisible man finally began to understand his purpose.

Chapter 2:
All I Want: The Currency of Heaven

The blue-white glow of the television flickered across Thomas Bradford's living room, casting shadows that danced along the walls lined with bookshelves. It was just past nine on a Tuesday evening, and Thomas had settled into his armchair with a cup of herbal tea, Edison curled at his feet. He hadn't intended to watch the celebrity interview show that now played before him, but after finishing his writing for the day, he'd turned on the TV for background noise while he rested his eyes.

The host—a polished woman with impossibly white teeth and a practiced laugh—was interviewing a tech billionaire whose name Thomas vaguely recognized from newspaper headlines. The man lounged in his designer suit, one leg crossed casually over the other, as he described his latest acquisitions.

"What do you still want to achieve?" the host asked, leaning forward with practiced interest.

The billionaire's eyes lit up as he began listing his desires: a second home in the Alps to complement his Malibu beach mansion, a larger yacht to replace his current 90-foot vessel, a private island, and expansion of his car collection which already included twelve vehicles that each cost more than Thomas's entire house.

"You can never have too much," the man said with a laugh that the audience dutifully echoed. "I've got big dreams, and I intend to make every one of them reality."

Thomas reached for the remote and pressed mute, silencing the billionaire's catalog of extravagance. Edison lifted his graying muzzle, sensing his master's shift in mood.

"How much is enough, Edison?" Thomas asked quietly, scratching behind the dog's ears. "When does 'more' stop mattering?"

It was a question that had occupied Thomas's thoughts frequently throughout his life, especially as he watched former classmates and colleagues chase promotions, larger houses, and status symbols. As an accountant, he had managed the finances of clients ranging from struggling small business owners to wealthy professionals, and he had observed firsthand the peculiar phenomenon that appeared regardless of income level: the persistent belief that happiness lay just beyond the next financial threshold.

"Make another hundred thousand, and then I'll be set," clients would tell him, only to move the goalpost once that mark was achieved. "Just need to hit a million in investments, then I can relax." But relaxation never came—only new desires, new targets, new acquisitions deemed essential for contentment.

Thomas rose from his chair, his knees protesting slightly after sitting too long, and walked to the window. The night was clear, stars visible despite the modest light pollution of Millfield. His neighborhood was firmly middle-class—not the wealthiest in town but far from struggling. The houses were well-maintained, lawns neatly trimmed, family sedans and SUVs parked in driveways.

His own modest ranch-style home had served him well for thirty years. He had paid off the mortgage fifteen years ago, a fact that gave him profound peace of mind during economic downturns. The furniture was comfortable if not fashionable, the appliances

9

functional though not the latest models. Thomas had always lived within his means, setting aside enough for retirement and the occasional small luxury like his annual fishing trip to Minnesota or the premium coffee beans he treated himself to each month.

"The thing is," Thomas said, turning back to Edison who watched him with devoted attention, "I've never seen anyone truly satisfied by accumulation. The more they get, the more they want, and the more they worry about losing what they have."

He thought about Harold Westfield, a client whose portfolio Thomas had managed for years before his retirement from the accounting firm. Harold owned three houses, each sitting empty most of the year, and spent more on security systems to protect his possessions than Thomas spent on all his living expenses combined. During their quarterly meetings, Harold would obsessively review every investment, panicking at the slightest market fluctuation, perpetually afraid that his wealth might somehow evaporate despite its vastness.

Thomas returned to his chair and picked up the leather-bound journal he'd started keeping since beginning work on his stories. He opened to a fresh page and wrote at the top: "All I Want." Below it, he began to explore his thoughts.

It seems counterintuitive, but I've observed that wealth often multiplies problems rather than solving them. The wealthy man frets over market volatility, property taxes, maintenance of possessions, the loyalty of friends who might value his resources more than his company. He builds higher walls, installs more security cameras, trusts fewer people. Is this the freedom that wealth supposedly brings?

Thomas paused, thinking about the billionaire on television. The man had spoken proudly about his charitable foundation, describing the millions he donated annually to various causes. The host had praised his generosity effusively, calling him a "true humanitarian."

There is nothing inherently wrong with charity, Thomas continued writing. Indeed, generosity is a virtue emphasized throughout Scripture. But Jesus saw through performative giving designed to enhance reputation rather than address genuine need. He praised the widow's humble mite above the ostentatious donations of the wealthy because her giving represented true sacrifice rather than excess disposal.

Matthew 6:2-4 comes to mind: "So when you give to the needy, do not announce it with trumpets, as the hypocrites do in the synagogues and on the streets, to be honored by others. Truly I tell you, they have received their reward in full. But when you give to the needy, do not let your left hand know what your right hand is doing, so that your giving may be in secret. Then your Father, who sees what is done in secret, will reward you."

Thomas remembered a small incident from his church a few years back. One of the wealthier members—a successful real estate developer—had donated a significant sum for the renovation of the fellowship hall. The man had insisted on a bronze plaque bearing his name and had mentioned his contribution in every church meeting for months afterward. Meanwhile, Mrs. Abernathy, an elderly widow living on a fixed income, quietly prepared meals for sick congregation members, drove people to medical appointments, and sent handwritten cards of encouragement—all without recognition or acknowledgment.

"Jesus never sought the company of the powerful or wealthy for their status," Thomas murmured as he continued writing. "When He did interact with the rich, it was often to challenge their attachment to worldly possessions, as with the rich young ruler who went away sorrowful when asked to sell his possessions and give to the poor."

Edison stirred at Thomas's feet and rose with difficulty, his arthritic hips making his movements deliberate. Thomas reached down to help the old dog onto the couch beside him, where Edison settled with a contented sigh.

"The company Jesus kept is telling, isn't it, boy?" Thomas said, stroking the dog's golden fur. "Fishermen, tax collectors, women of questionable reputation, the sick, the outcasts. Not exactly the social elite of first-century Palestine."

Thomas thought about how Jesus conducted His ministry—healing the sick, restoring sight to the blind, cleansing lepers—often followed by instructions not to tell anyone who had performed the miracle. It wasn't about building a personal brand or accumulating followers. It was about fulfilling His Father's will, doing good for its own sake rather than for recognition.

The contrast with modern influencer culture could not be starker. Thomas had recently heard a sermon about how some churches were employing marketing tactics to increase attendance, focusing more on entertainment value than spiritual depth. The message had troubled him deeply.

Salvation is not achieved through humanitarian works or being a "good person," Thomas wrote. The rich man who obediently followed all commandments still lacked the one thing necessary—

surrender of his heart's primary allegiance. "No one comes to the Father except through Me," Jesus declared, establishing Himself as the exclusive pathway to reconciliation with God.

Thomas closed his journal and leaned back in his chair, thinking about his own relationship with material possessions. He had never been wealthy, but neither had he experienced true poverty. His needs had always been met, though there had been seasons of careful budgeting and delayed gratification.

In his twenties, fresh out of college and starting his accounting career, Thomas had briefly aspired to the trappings of success his peers pursued—the luxury car, the designer clothes, the trendy downtown apartment. He had even taken out a loan for a sports car he couldn't really afford, believing it might somehow make him more visible, more worthy of attention.

Three months of stressful payments later, Thomas had sold the car at a loss and returned to his reliable, paid-off sedan. The experience had been a valuable lesson in the hollow promises of material acquisition. The car had not made him happier, had not filled the void of his invisibility. If anything, it had added anxiety to his life without providing any meaningful return.

"We bring nothing into this world, and we take nothing out," Thomas quoted softly, remembering the passage from 1 Timothy that had often provided perspective during moments of material temptation.

Rising from his chair, Thomas walked to the small writing desk in the corner of his living room where he had been working on his stories. His laptop sat closed, tomorrow's writing session already planned. He had been making steady progress on his collection of biblical retellings, finding his voice growing stronger with each completed piece.

Thomas opened a drawer and pulled out a small wooden box, a gift from his father on his college graduation day. Inside was a collection of items that held personal significance—not valuable by any market standard but priceless to Thomas. His father's pocket watch, a pressed wildflower from a hiking trip in the Rockies where Thomas had felt particularly close to God, a small cross carved from olive wood that a church friend had brought back from Jerusalem, and a photograph of his parents on their wedding day.

These treasures would have no place in a billionaire's vault, yet they represented what Thomas valued most—connection, memory, faith, beauty found in simplicity.

"Jesus didn't even have a place to lay His head," Thomas whispered, carefully returning the box to its drawer. "The Creator of all things walked this earth in humble circumstances, demonstrating that true wealth has nothing to do with possessions."

Thomas thought about his writing project—his collection of stories that explored the lives of biblical figures who had encountered Christ. In each narrative, the transformation never came through material gain but through spiritual awakening, through recognizing Jesus as the pearl of great price worth trading everything else to obtain.

"That's what I want readers to understand," Thomas said to Edison, who watched him with drowsy eyes. "When Jesus is all you have, you discover He's all you need."

The next morning, Thomas woke before his alarm, ideas for his chapter flowing freely. He made his coffee and settled at his desk while dawn light gradually brightened his window. His fingers moved steadily across the keyboard as he developed his thoughts on contentment, materialism, and the sufficiency of Christ.

I've observed the wealthy who appear to have everything yet possess profound spiritual poverty, he wrote. And I've known those of modest means whose lives overflow with joy and peace because they have found their treasure in Christ.

When I'm tempted by the newest gadget advertised on television or feel that momentary envy at someone's vacation photos from exotic locations, I try to pause and ask myself: Is this something I want, or something I need? Will this purchase draw me closer to God or distract me from His presence? Will it simplify my life or complicate it with maintenance, insurance, storage, and worry?

Thomas stopped typing and looked out his window. Mrs. Pemberton from next door was walking her small terrier, waving when she noticed Thomas in the window. He waved back, smiling. Community, connection, simple kindness—these were currencies of heaven that no bank could hold.

I'm not suggesting we should never enjoy material blessings or that poverty itself is inherently virtuous, Thomas continued. God delights in providing for His children. But the constant pursuit of more—more money, more status, more possessions—reveals a hunger that material acquisition can never satisfy.

All I truly want and need is Jesus—His presence, His guidance, His love that transcends circumstance. In Him, I find my identity, not in what I own or how I'm perceived by others. In Him, I discover my purpose, not in climbing corporate ladders or accumulating status symbols. In Him, I secure my eternity, not through charitable donations or public acclaim but through simple faith in His finished work on the cross.

Thomas worked through the morning, expanding his reflections into a cohesive chapter that wove together personal observations, biblical principles, and gentle challenges to cultural assumptions about success and fulfillment. By noon, when Edison nudged his leg as a reminder of their daily walk, Thomas had completed a first draft that felt authentic and meaningful.

As they strolled through the neighborhood, Thomas noticed things he might have missed if his mind had been preoccupied with acquisition and status—the cardinal singing from the maple tree, the wild violets pushing through cracks in the sidewalk, the sound of children laughing in a backyard. These simple pleasures required no wealth to enjoy, no status to access.

"The kingdom of heaven is like treasure hidden in a field," Thomas quoted softly as they turned toward home. "When a man found it, he hid it again, and then in his joy went and sold all he had and bought that field."

All he wanted—all he truly needed—was the treasure he had already found.

Chapter 3:
When Rain Falls: A Mother's Legacy

Thomas Bradford sat at his kitchen table, a blank sheet of stationery before him, pen held motionless above the pristine page. Outside, a gentle spring rain tapped against the window panes, creating a soothing rhythm that contrasted with the storm of emotions within him. Edison lay at his feet, occasionally lifting his graying muzzle to offer silent companionship.

Today marked one year since his mother, Eleanor Bradford, had passed away. One year since he had stood in the driveway of her modest home, watching as attendants from Miller's Funeral Home had carefully loaded her earthly remains into their vehicle. One year of adjustment to a world without her steadying presence.

Thomas placed the pen down and reached for the well-worn leather journal beside him. He opened it to a letter he had written but never sent—composed in the raw, immediate aftermath of her passing. The pages were slightly wrinkled in places where tears had fallen during its writing.

Dear Mom, I am writing you this letter because today is Wednesday, the 22nd of May 2024. This morning around 11 a.m., you went home to be with the Lord. While I will miss you and think about you constantly, I find comfort knowing you are in a place where there is no more sadness, no more pain, and no more worries. It makes my grief more bearable, understanding that I will be joining you someday. I want you to know that I am profoundly blessed to have had you as my mother. You were the sweetest, kindest, gentlest, most Christian person I have ever known. I would not be the man I am today if it weren't for your influence.

Thomas paused in his reading, remembering the morning of his mother's passing. He had received the call from his brother just after 10:30 a.m. "Mr. Bradford, I think you should come right away. Your mother has taken a turn." By the time he had arrived, slightly out of breath from having parked hastily and rushed inside, she was already gone—her departure as quiet and unassuming as the way she had lived. She had been on hospice care at home.

The nurses had told him she had been lucid that morning, had eaten a light breakfast, and had asked to sit by the window to watch the birds at the feeder Thomas had installed outside her room. She had been reading her Bible—the same one she had received as a confirmation gift at twelve years old, its pages now thin with use, margins filled with her neat handwriting—when she had simply closed her eyes and slipped away.

Thomas continued reading his letter, his voice a whisper in the empty kitchen.

I know that we fought sometimes over trivial matters that were invariably my fault. I am deeply sorry for the way I made you feel because I wanted immediate gratification or insisted on having things my way. When all was said and done, 99.999% of the time, you were right. You weathered some extraordinarily difficult circumstances—a painful divorce that left us to fend for ourselves, after which you secured employment at San Juan College where you dedicated twenty-five years of service and were rightfully inducted into the SJC Hall of Fame. Then you endured the losses of two husbands after that: Jim and Roy. You now rest peacefully beside Roy, as you wished.

Eleanor Bradford had never been one to dwell on hardships, though her life had presented many. Thomas remembered the night his father had left—he was twelve years old, awakened by hushed, tense voices followed by the sound of a suitcase being dragged down the hallway and the decisive slam of the front door. The following morning, his mother had appeared at breakfast with reddened eyes but a resolute expression.

"Things will be different now," she had told Thomas. "But we're going to be fine. God has never abandoned us, and He's not about to start now."

Within a week, she had secured a position as an administrative assistant at San Juan College, despite having been out of the workforce for fifteen years. She had risen through the ranks over the decades, eventually becoming the director of student services, beloved by faculty and students alike for her compassionate approach and unwavering integrity.

Thomas's eyes returned to the letter.

You were consistently present throughout every challenge I faced. You stood by my side through all my surgical procedures—from my eyes to my neck, both shoulders, both hands, my abdomen twice, and my knee. I believe that covers the inventory. You were there every step of the way—before each procedure, during the process, and throughout my recovery. You exemplified what it means to be a parent, though I failed to recognize it during my formative years. Your character and values gradually influenced me, shaping me into a better person than I might otherwise have become.

His mother had indeed been his most steadfast advocate during health crises. Thomas unconsciously rubbed his left shoulder, where arthritis now reminded him of the rotator cuff surgery he had undergone in his forties. Eleanor had temporarily moved into his spare bedroom during his recovery, cooking meals that could be eaten one-handed, helping with laundry, and driving him to physical therapy appointments three times weekly without a single complaint.

"That's what mothers do," she had said simply when he had tried to express his gratitude.

As I stood in the front yard of your home watching them load your body into the mortuary van, I experienced a moment of profound realization—that was merely your earthly vessel, an empty shell. Your essence, your spirit, is no longer here. You are with Jesus in paradise. From everything Scripture tells us about Heaven, I can only imagine your delight in its splendors. Although I miss you tremendously and will carry an ache in my heart until we meet again, I find solace in knowing I will join you there someday.

After all that has been said, I simply want to express: I LOVE YOU, MOM Your son, Thomas

Thomas closed the journal, his fingers lingering on its cover. He had never sent the letter, of course—it had been written after her passing, a therapeutic exercise suggested by Pastor Jenkins when Thomas had sought counsel in his grief. But the sentiments expressed remained as true today as they had been in those first raw hours of loss.

Eleanor Bradford had been a woman of remarkable resilience and unshakable faith. She was born in 1936 in Oklahoma and moved to New Mexico for the oil and gas industry. She had grown up with modest means but abundant love. Her father had worked in the copper mines, coming home exhausted but never too tired to listen to Eleanor read from her school books or play simple hymns on their secondhand piano. Her mother had managed their household with resourceful creativity, making dresses from flour sacks and turning leftover roast into savory stews that could stretch for days.

These early lessons in frugality and finding joy in simplicity had served Eleanor well when her husband of seventeen years had abruptly declared their marriage "a mistake" and departed with his administrative assistant from the insurance agency where he had worked. Left with two children, a mortgage, and minimal child support that often arrived late if at all, Eleanor had modeled dignity and determination for Thomas and his brother.

"We never want for what truly matters," she would say when they couldn't afford the trendy clothes or expensive outings their peers enjoyed. "We have each other, a roof over our heads, food on our table, and God's grace. Everything else is just extra."

Her faith had been the foundation of their home—not expressed in rigid religiosity or judgmental pronouncements but in quiet daily practices. Eleanor read her Bible each morning before dawn, prayers shaping her day before it began. She taught Sunday School for over thirty years, her gentle approach drawing even the most reluctant children into engagement with biblical stories. When Thomas had gone through a period of spiritual questioning in college, she had listened without defensiveness, affirming that honest doubt often led to deeper faith.

"God's shoulders are broad enough to carry your questions," she had told him. "He's not intimidated by your uncertainty."

Thomas rose from the table and moved to the living room window, watching raindrops chase each other down the glass. His mother had loved rainy days, calling them "God's garden service" and often sitting on her covered porch during storms, a cup of tea in hand, simply observing nature's display.

Five years after his father's departure, Eleanor had married Jim Reynolds, a kind widower who taught physics at the college. For eight years, they had shared a content partnership until pancreatic cancer had claimed him with devastating swiftness. Thomas had watched his mother nurse Jim through his final months with tender attention to every detail of his comfort, never betraying the exhaustion she must have felt.

Three years later, to everyone's surprise including her own, Eleanor had found love again with Roy Hendricks, a retired forest ranger with a deep laugh and gentle hands that coaxed extraordinary blooms from ordinary garden plants. They had enjoyed fifteen years together before Roy's heart had given out while they were walking their beloved beagle, Max, one autumn evening.

"God keeps giving me men to love," Eleanor had said at Roy's funeral, her voice steady despite her grief. "And then He calls them home before me. I have to believe there's purpose in that pattern, even if I can't see it clearly now."

Thomas's reflections were interrupted by Edison's soft whine. The old dog needed his afternoon walk, rain or shine. Thomas smiled, grateful for the companionship that eased his solitude.

"Just like Mom's dogs, aren't you?" he said, reaching for Edison's leash. "Keeping me on schedule, making sure I don't get too lost in my head."

Eleanor had always had a dog, from Thomas's earliest memories until her final days. She claimed they were the best teachers of unconditional love outside of Christ Himself. Her last companion, a gentle cocker spaniel named Lady, had been inconsolable after Eleanor's passing, refusing food until Thomas had brought her home to live with him and Edison. Lady had rallied briefly but had passed away three months later.

"Died of a broken heart," the veterinarian had said, not entirely joking.

As Thomas and Edison ventured into the light spring rain, he reflected on the complicated nature of grief—how it ebbed and flowed, sometimes catching him unaware in ordinary moments. Just last week, he had found himself reaching for the phone to call his mother after finishing a particularly challenging chapter of his writing project, forgetting momentarily that she was no longer there to offer her thoughtful feedback.

The rain intensified, and Thomas quickened their pace, guiding Edison back toward home. Once inside, he toweled off the dog's damp fur and prepared a fresh cup of tea. Returning to his writing desk, he opened his laptop and created a new document.

For months, he had been working on his collection of biblical narratives, giving voice to overlooked or minimized characters in Scripture. But today, on this anniversary, a different type of story called to him—one drawn from his own experience, exploring the enduring impact of a mother's love and faith through life's vicissitudes.

Thomas had not originally planned to include personal elements in his book. His invisibility had conditioned him to believe his own story held little interest for others. But as his fingers began moving across the keyboard, he realized that his mother's story—their story—contained universal elements that might resonate with readers. The themes of enduring faith amid hardship, of finding purpose in pain, of love's transformative power—these transcended his particular circumstances.

He began writing, the words flowing with unexpected ease: We never truly know our parents until we view them through adult eyes. As children, we see them primarily in relation to ourselves—as providers, rule-makers, comforters, or sources of frustration. Only with maturity and distance do we begin to perceive them as complete human beings with histories, dreams, and identities separate from their parental roles.

My mother, Eleanor Grace Bradford (née), was fifty-three years old when I first really saw her...

Thomas wrote through the afternoon and into the evening, pausing only to feed Edison and make a simple dinner for himself. He traced his mother's journey from her childhood in mining-town New Mexico through her education at the state university (the first in her family to attend college), her marriage and motherhood, the devastating abandonment by his father, and her reinvention as a single working mother. He detailed her career achievements, her service to church and community, her later marriages and widowhoods, and finally, her dignified navigation of aging and illness.

Throughout the narrative, Thomas highlighted the consistent thread that had defined Eleanor's life: her unshakable faith that had sustained her through circumstances that might have broken a person of lesser spiritual fortitude. He described how her example had shaped his own relationship with God, even during periods when he had questioned or struggled.

As midnight approached, Thomas finally saved his work and closed his laptop. The chapter would need revision and polishing, but the essence was there—a son's tribute to a mother whose quiet strength had shaped him more profoundly than he had recognized until her absence had clarified her influence.

Thomas prepared for bed, completing his nightly routine with the methodical thoroughness that had been one of many habits inherited from his mother. As he settled under the covers, Edison taking his customary place at the foot of the bed, Thomas offered a simple prayer of gratitude.

"Thank you, Lord, for the gift of Eleanor Bradford," he whispered into the darkness. "For her love, her example, and the legacy she left that continues to shape me. And thank you for the assurance that our separation is temporary, that one day—in Your perfect timing—we will be reunited in Your presence."

Outside, the rain had stopped. Moonlight filtered through parting clouds, casting silver patterns on the bedroom wall. Thomas drifted toward sleep, comforted by the memory of his mother's favorite Scripture passage from Romans: "For I am convinced that neither death nor life, neither angels nor demons, neither the present nor the future, nor any powers, neither height nor depth, nor anything else in all creation, will be able to separate us from the love of God that is in Christ Jesus our Lord."

Not even death could sever that connection—or the bond between a mother and son forged through decades of love and shared faith. In that assurance, Thomas found peace.

Chapter 4:
Inheritance of Doubt: My Father's Legacy

It feels almost sacrilegious to continue this narrative without turning my thoughts, heavy and complex as they are, toward my dad. In the intricate tapestry of my life, his thread is undeniably dark in places, yet it's woven so tightly that its absence would leave a gaping hole. For a significant portion of my childhood, the image I held in his mind, or at least the one he projected, was that of an unfortunate mishap, a blip in his plans. My earliest memories are often tinged with the subtle, and sometimes not-so-subtle, implication that I was simply not up to par.

My dad was a mechanic, a man who understood the intricate dance of gears and engines, the precise torque of a wrench. Naturally, he attempted to pass this practical knowledge onto his son. The garage, with its pungent aroma of oil and gasoline, the scattered tools gleaming under the harsh fluorescent light, became my reluctant classroom. But where he saw potential, he often found only frustration in me. Every fumbled tool, every incorrectly identified part, seemed to chip away at his patience. The exasperated sighs, the tightened jaw, the eventual pronouncement, "Let me do it before you break it," or the dismissive, "We don't have time for this," became a recurring soundtrack to my young life. These weren't just isolated incidents; they were persistent whispers that burrowed deep, programming me with a profound lack of confidence in my own abilities. To this day, that ingrained feeling of inadequacy lingers, a shadow that follows me as I approach even the simplest tasks, often necessitating a call for help.

Then, when I was thirteen, the already fragile foundation of our family fractured irrevocably. My dad found solace, or perhaps simply a new path, in the arms of another woman. He left, abruptly and decisively, leaving my mom, my brother, and me adrift in a sea of confusion and abandonment. For a long time, a bitter resentment festered within me, a toxic brew of hurt and anger that threatened to consume me from the inside out. Those raw, unprocessed feelings were a constant weight, a leaden cloak I carried through my days. But one day, in a moment of quiet introspection, a profound sense of clarity washed over me. It felt, undeniably, like a divine whisper, a gentle but firm voice telling me that holding onto such negativity was a self-inflicted wound. "Let it all go," the voice seemed to say. "It's just not worth it." And in that moment, I knew, with a certainty that resonated deep within my soul, that God was right. He always is. I made the conscious decision to release the corrosive grip of that resentment, to try and find a space of neutrality, if not understanding, within my heart.

Life, as it so often does, continued its relentless march forward. Fast forward to May of 2024, a month etched in my memory with the sharp pain of loss. That was when we said goodbye to Mom. Her illness had been a slow, agonizing decline, each day stealing a little more of her vibrant spirit. I stood witness to this heartbreaking erosion, feeling helpless as the inevitable drew closer. My brother, I realize now with a sense of awe, possessed a strength I didn't fully comprehend at the time. He saw more, understood more, navigated the treacherous terrain of her illness with a quiet fortitude that still leaves me humbled.

And then, the narrative took another unexpected turn. My dad, too, had been battling his own health issues, though the gravity of his condition remained largely unknown to me. Just a month after we laid Mom to rest, he passed away as well. In the time leading up to his death, he had expressed a desire to speak with my brother and me. But we were both emotionally drained, weary of the sterile scent of hospitals, the hushed whispers of concerned relatives, the crushing weight of mortality. The recent loss of Mom had left us raw, and the prospect of facing another impending death felt like an unbearable burden. We made the difficult decision not to go.

Even now, months later, a persistent unease gnaws at me. Did we make the right choice? The question echoes in the quiet moments, a haunting refrain in the soundtrack of my thoughts. And if I'm truly honest with myself, beyond the exhaustion and the grief, I have to acknowledge that the old, buried feelings toward my dad likely played a part in that decision. A flicker of that old resentment, perhaps, or simply a weariness of navigating the complexities of our relationship. Admitting that sting of lingering hard feelings is difficult, a truth I've tried to sidestep, but it sits there nonetheless, a quiet testament to the enduring impact of the past. The silence of those final days with him remains a heavy weight, a chapter left unwritten, a conversation forever lost.

Chapter 5:
The Enigma of Endowment:
Why Some Soar While Others Stumble

The human condition is a landscape of stark contrasts, a vibrant mosaic where some tiles gleam with seemingly effortless brilliance while others appear muted, their purpose less immediately apparent. It's a contemplation that has often occupied the quiet corners of my mind: this perplexing distribution of talent, this seemingly arbitrary bestowal of gifts. Why does one person's touch transform a canvas into a breathtaking vista, while another struggles to sketch a recognizable form? Why does melody flow with such natural grace from one set of fingers, while another fumbles across the keys? And why do some navigate the complexities of life with an innate aptitude for success, while others, like myself, often feel as though they are perpetually searching for the right path?

Our church provides a weekly testament to this fascinating disparity. I stand in awe as our pianist's hands dance across the ivory and ebony, a fluid ballet that conjures melodies capable of stirring the deepest emotions within us. Each note is precise, each chord resonant, a testament to a gift so profound it feels almost otherworldly. Then there's our worship leader, whose voice possesses a similar magic. The sheer power and beauty of their singing can elevate the entire congregation, creating a palpable sense of connection and reverence. It's a talent so undeniable, so captivating, that it leaves me breathless.

Beyond the sanctuary walls, I witness this phenomenon in the lives of those around me. I have a dear friend, a nurse, whose intellect and dedication to her profession are truly astounding. She possesses a sharp, analytical mind that has contributed to groundbreaking medical projects, her knowledge a vast and intricate web of understanding. To listen to her speak about her work is to enter a realm of complex science that leaves my own comprehension far behind.

Then I look at my own family, and the contrast becomes even more personal. My brother, for instance, possesses a remarkable dexterity and an artistic eye. He can effortlessly translate his visions onto canvas, construct intricate models with painstaking precision, and even coax life back into ailing vehicles. He seems to possess an innate understanding of how things work, how they fit together, how to bring ideas into tangible form.

And then there's me. My attempts at drawing resemble the chaotic scribbles of a toddler. My forays into the world of construction invariably end in lopsided disasters and a pile of unusable materials. And as for anything mechanical, I am, without exaggeration, a complete moron. It's a frustrating reality, especially considering our father's profession. He was a skilled mechanic, his hands capable of diagnosing and repairing the most stubborn engine problems. Yet, this aptitude seemed to skip a generation, leaving me utterly bewildered by the simplest mechanical tasks. Genetics, I understand, plays a role, but it still feels like a cosmic joke.

I know, intellectually at least, that there's a divine plan for each of us, a unique purpose woven into the fabric of our existence. But for someone like me, who has spent so much time feeling utterly lost in terms of vocation, that understanding can be a source of both comfort and profound frustration. It's like knowing there's a destination, but constantly feeling like you're holding the wrong map, or perhaps no map at all.

This has been a subject of fervent prayer for me, a persistent question I've laid before the Almighty countless times. And knowing my own tendency to be oblivious, it's entirely possible that He has tried to guide me, to whisper my purpose into my ear, and I've simply been too preoccupied or too dense to hear. I've dabbled in various pursuits, hoping to stumble upon that elusive "calling," that one thing that would ignite a spark of passion and competence within me.

Interestingly, there was one arena where I did find a measure of success, a brief period where I felt a sense of belonging: the world of radio. For nearly two decades, I was a DJ, a voice on the airwaves. In that realm, my primary task was simply to play music and, if I'm being honest, engage in a fair amount of lighthearted mischief that probably wasn't strictly in the job description. It was fun, undeniably so, a period of relative ease and enjoyment. Yet, it was also during this time that I began to drift away from my faith, my compass spinning off course.

It was the persistent and loving nudges of my mother that eventually steered me back toward the familiar comfort of the church. For that, I remain eternally grateful. But even now, as I sit in the pews and witness the extraordinary talents of others, that old question resurfaces: why this seemingly uneven distribution of gifts? Why does it appear that some are blessed with such obvious and impactful abilities, while others seem to wander through life without a clear, discernible talent?

And yet, I return to the fundamental truth I try to hold onto: He has a plan for us all, whether that plan is immediately apparent or remains shrouded in mystery. His timing is not ours; His perspective transcends our limited understanding. The pianist's gift blesses our worship, the singer's voice lifts our spirits, the nurse's intellect heals and advances knowledge. My brother's creativity brings beauty into the world. And perhaps, in my own journey of searching, in my moments of feeling inadequate, there is a purpose too. Perhaps the path isn't always about possessing a singular, dazzling talent, but about the experiences we gather, the lessons we learn, and the empathy we develop along the way.

So, the only true recourse is patience. To trust in the unseen hand that guides us, even when the direction feels unclear. He is with us, in our moments of brilliance and in our times of feeling utterly ordinary. And perhaps, in the grand tapestry of life, the seemingly muted threads are just as essential, their purpose revealed not in a singular burst of talent, but in the intricate pattern they help to create.

Chapter 6:
The Unsung and the Divine:
My Personal Pantheon of Heroes

Throughout the winding narrative of my life, I've been fortunate enough to encounter individuals who, in their own profound ways, embody the very essence of a hero. The concept of heroism, I've come to realize, extends far beyond the grand gestures and mythical tales we often associate with the word. It lives in the quiet acts of resilience, the unwavering dedication to duty, and the selfless sacrifices made for something far greater than oneself.

In my eyes, anyone who chooses to put on a uniform and serve our nation is a hero, especially those who have faced the crucible of combat. Their commitment to protecting our freedoms, often at immense personal risk, is a testament to a courage that few possess. My stepfather, Roy, was one such hero. Part of that remarkable "Greatest Generation," he fought in the Philippines during World War II. He rarely spoke of the horrors he witnessed, but the quiet strength and unwavering sense of duty that radiated from him left an indelible mark on me. In my young eyes, and even now, he was unequivocally a hero.

Yet, heroism isn't always found on the battlefield. Sometimes, it resides in the tireless efforts and boundless love of an ordinary person facing extraordinary challenges. My mother, Norma, never wore a military uniform or engaged in armed conflict. But if heroism is defined by selfless dedication, unwavering strength, and the relentless pursuit of another's well-being, then my mom was a hero in the truest sense. Raising my brother and me as a single parent, navigating the turbulent waters of our childhood and adolescence, enduring our youthful antics, and working tirelessly to keep food on our table – that, to me, is a monumental act of heroism. Her quiet determination, her boundless love, and her sheer resilience in the face of daily struggles were a constant source of strength for us.

Beyond the realms of military service and parental sacrifice, I've also found heroes in the vibrant world of rock and roll, the soundtrack to so much of my life. Def Leppard, with their electrifying energy, has always been a major one for me. Sammy Hagar, with his infectious enthusiasm during his time with Van Halen, is another. And Benjamin Orr of The Cars, with his smooth, distinctive voice, offered a different kind of musical heroism. These artists, through their ability to create, inspire, and connect with audiences on a deep emotional level, shaped my experiences and gave voice to feelings I couldn't always articulate.

I've heard countless stories of heroes of all kinds – the ordinary person who, in a moment of crisis, rises to extraordinary heights of courage and selflessness. The athletes who push beyond perceived limits, inspiring millions with their dedication and perseverance. There are unsung heroes everywhere: military personnel in vital support roles, everyday citizens who step in to help a neighbor in need, quiet volunteers who simply want to make their communities better. They often fly under the radar, their acts of valor unseen by the wider world, yet their impact is no less significant.

But towering above all these earthly heroes, the one whose heroism transcends every other, is my Lord and Savior, Jesus Christ. His sacrifice on the cross, His death and glorious resurrection, represents the ultimate act of love and redemption. Through His grace, a free gift offered to all who believe, I have found salvation. As He Himself declared in John 14:6, "I am the way, the truth, and the life. No one comes to the Father except through me." The path to eternal life is open to all who seek it, who acknowledge their need for forgiveness

and invite Jesus into their lives. This simple act of faith initiates a profound transformation, a spiritual rebirth into a new life with the promise of eternity, a truth beautifully encapsulated in the powerful words of John 3:16.

These are just some of my thoughts on heroism. The concept continues to evolve and expand in my understanding. Perhaps the most profound realization is this: you, an ordinary everyday person, have the potential to be a hero to somebody. It doesn't require grand gestures or public acclaim. Often, the most impactful acts of heroism are the quiet, unseen gestures of kindness, compassion, and support. Just as Jesus performed many miracles and then quietly faded back into the crowd, allowing His actions to speak for themselves, we too can be heroes in the lives of those around us without seeking recognition.

So, be a hero to someone. You may never truly know the profound impact of your seemingly small act of valor.

Chapter 7:
Whispers in the Static:
Deconstructing the Myth of Ghosts

The fascination with the spectral, the lingering presence of those who have departed this earthly realm, is a thread that runs deep through the fabric of human culture. From ancient folklore to modern television, the notion of ghosts – the disembodied spirits of the deceased tethered to our world – holds a persistent grip on our collective imagination. I can certainly understand the allure, the compelling mystery that fuels countless paranormal investigations and late-night storytelling sessions. The very idea of peering beyond the veil, of glimpsing some vestige of a life lived, is undeniably intriguing.

The proliferation of television shows dedicated to "ghost hunting" and attempting to communicate with these supposed apparitions speaks volumes about this widespread fascination. Armed with an array of technological gadgets, these intrepid explorers venture into shadowy locales, hoping to capture a flicker of movement, a disembodied voice, some tangible evidence of a spirit's presence. I suppose there's a certain captivating drama in these endeavors, a tantalizing possibility that the boundaries between worlds might be thinner than we perceive.

However, when I turn to the bedrock of my faith, the Holy Bible, a different perspective emerges, one that offers a clear and definitive stance on the nature of spirits. Scripture unequivocally states the existence of spirit beings, both benevolent and malevolent – angels, the messengers of God, and demons, fallen angels aligned with darkness. But the concept of human spirits lingering on Earth as ghosts, haunting the living, finds no support within its pages.

In fact, I believe that what many perceive as ghosts are, in reality, something far more insidious: the deceptive machinations of demons. These malevolent entities, driven by their desire to mislead and draw humanity away from God, are masters of disguise. What could be more effective than masquerading as the familiar spirit of a deceased loved one?

The profound grief and longing that accompany loss create a fertile ground for such deception. A person yearning to connect with a departed spouse, parent, or child might be particularly vulnerable to believing a demonic entity that cleverly mimics the voice, mannerisms, or even appearance they so desperately crave.

The book of Hebrews offers a powerful counterpoint to the notion of lingering human spirits. Hebrews 9:27 plainly states, "And just as each person is destined to die once, and after that to face judgment." This verse lays out a clear trajectory: life, death, and then judgment. There is no intermediate state of earthly wandering for human souls. For the believer, the outcome of that judgment is eternal life in heaven; for the unbeliever, it is separation from God in hell. There is no biblical basis for a purgatorial limbo where spirits remain earthbound as ghosts.

The spiritual realm is indeed active and capable of interacting with our world, but the players are angels and demons, not the lingering souls of the departed. Angels, the forces of good, serve God and often intervene in human affairs according to His will. Demons, on the other hand, are the embodiment of evil, constantly seeking opportunities to deceive, corrupt, and lead people astray from the path of righteousness. Their ultimate goal is to drag as many souls down to their level, into the darkness that separates them from God's light.

This is why the Bible emphasizes the crucial importance of Christians staying rooted in the Word of God and maintaining a consistent practice of prayer. These are our primary defenses against the deceptive tactics of demons. They recoil from the light of truth and the power of prayer. When we immerse ourselves in Scripture and communicate directly with God, we build an impenetrable shield against their influence. They thrive in ignorance and spiritual apathy, seeking to exploit our weaknesses and lead us down paths that deviate from God's will.

I will admit, with a touch of sheepishness, that I too have occasionally succumbed to the allure of those ghost-hunting television shows. However, my engagement has always been purely for entertainment value, a fleeting curiosity about the unexplained. After a few episodes, the formulaic nature and the often-tenuous evidence tend to lose their appeal.

My more enduring fascination lies in the realm of the cryptid, the elusive creatures that skirt the edges of our known world, like Bigfoot. Again, this is primarily for entertainment, a playful exploration of the mysteries that still elude scientific explanation.

There is undoubtedly a vast amount in this world that remains beyond my comprehension, and perhaps that is by divine design. Not every mystery is meant to be solved by human intellect. However, when it comes to the phenomenon of ghosts, I feel a firm conviction in the truth revealed in Scripture. I believe I understand their true nature. Perhaps this inherent curiosity, this desire to unravel the unknown, is itself a gift from God, prompting us to seek knowledge and understanding, even if the answers sometimes lie within the pages of a book rather than in the flickering shadows of a haunted house.

So, my counsel remains steadfast: stay anchored in the Word of God, the ultimate source of truth and guidance, and don't succumb to fear or unfounded beliefs. Instead, bring all your concerns, all your questions, to God in prayer. He is our ultimate protector, our guiding light in a world filled with both seen and unseen forces.

Who you gonna call? Not ghost hunters with their gadgets and theories. The answer, unequivocally, is God. He is the one who holds the true answers, the one who offers genuine protection, and the one who illuminates the path of truth in a world often shrouded in shadows and deception.

Chapter 8:
The Divine Tapestry of Difference:
Finding Purpose in God's Design

The human mind, in its ceaseless quest for understanding, often grapples with the apparent disparities we observe in the world around us. Why are some individuals blessed with an abundance of talent in various fields, while others seem to possess a more modest share? Why do some radiate a captivating beauty, while others blend more seamlessly into the background? And why does intellectual prowess shine so brightly in some, while others navigate the world with a more grounded, practical intelligence? These are questions that have echoed in the chambers of my own mind, prompting moments of contemplation and a deeper search for meaning.

The intricacies of human variation become particularly poignant when observed within the close confines of a family. How can siblings, sharing the same genetic heritage and upbringing, diverge so dramatically in their aptitudes and inclinations? One might blossom into a celebrated athlete, their body a finely tuned instrument of grace and power, while their brother or sister might possess no discernible athletic inclination whatsoever. My own relationship with my brother serves as a vivid illustration of this phenomenon. Separated by a decade, with me as the elder, the distribution of inherent talents within our family seemed strikingly uneven. He inherited a remarkable dexterity and a creative spirit that manifests in his ability to paint captivating scenes, construct intricate models with meticulous detail, and even troubleshoot and repair his own vehicles with a confident expertise that I can only envy.

In stark contrast, my own attempts at artistic expression are laughably crude. My lines are never straight, even with the aid of a ruler. The mere thought of assembling anything beyond the simplest instructions fills me with a sense of impending doom. And the inner workings of an automobile remain a profound and impenetrable mystery.

The source of my brother's artistic and practical gifts, I believe, can be traced back to our mom. She was a woman of considerable talent, her fingers dancing effortlessly across the keys of a piano or organ, filling our home with music. She possessed a knack for intricate model building, completing projects that invariably left me bewildered and defeated. Even her handwriting was a form of art, each letter flowing with an elegant precision that resembled calligraphy. In comparison, my own penmanship has stubbornly remained at a third-grade level, a constant reminder of my own perceived lack of inherent artistic flair.

I understand, on an intellectual level, that God has a purpose in bestowing different gifts upon different people. There's a divine orchestration at play, a grand design where each individual contributes their unique notes to the symphony of life. Yet, there are times when I yearn to understand the specific rationale behind this distribution of talents. What's the underlying wisdom in granting such seemingly disparate abilities? For someone like me, who has often felt adrift in a sea of perceived inadequacies, the desire to know my own inherent strengths, my own unique contribution, can be particularly strong.

The one area where I experienced a genuine sense of competence and even a degree of success was in the realm of radio. For nearly two decades, I found my niche as a DJ, my voice resonating across the airwaves. There was a certain ease and enjoyment in selecting music, connecting with listeners, and even engaging in a bit of lighthearted banter.

However, the relentless march of technological progress eventually left me feeling like a relic of a bygone era, the digital landscape evolving at a pace I couldn't quite keep up with. I guess that's simply an inevitable part of the aging process, a reminder that the world continues to turn, often leaving us feeling slightly out of step.

Despite these moments of questioning and the occasional pang of wishing for different inherent abilities, my faith in God remains my steadfast anchor. I hold onto the unwavering belief that there's a purpose for each of us, a role to play in His grand design. Perhaps the talents we readily observe in others are merely one facet of a much larger picture. Maybe the true measure of our worth lies not solely in our innate abilities, but in our character, our resilience, and our willingness to trust in a plan that extends beyond our immediate understanding.

And so, I continue to keep my faith and trust in God. I believe that in His perfect timing, the purpose for my own life will become clearer. Perhaps the journey itself, the searching and the questioning, is an integral part of that purpose. One day, I may just discover the unique contribution I am meant to make, the specific way in which I am designed to serve and to glorify Him. Until then, I find solace in the knowledge that His love is unwavering, His plan is perfect, and that even in our differences, we are all integral parts of His magnificent creation.

Chapter 9:
The Blurring Lines: Navigating the Murky Waters of a Desensitized World

Our recent Sunday school discussion left me with a familiar unease, a disquieting reflection on the shifting sands of our cultural landscape. The topic at hand was the apparent desensitization of today's youth to the barrage of intense imagery that floods our screens – television, movies, video games. It's a stark contrast to my own childhood, a time when the visual narratives presented to us were far more restrained, leaving much to the theater of our own imaginations. I recall that even the simulated violence of a Western shootout or a police drama was largely bloodless. A figure would clutch their chest, perhaps utter a pained groan, and then simply fall. The aftermath was implied, not graphically displayed.

Today, however, the visual language of violence has become increasingly explicit, almost gratuitous. A gunshot wound is no longer a clean, abstract event. It's often depicted with visceral detail – the crimson spray, the contorted features, the lingering aftermath of brutality. And that, as I see it, is often considered "mild" in the spectrum of what's readily available.

The cinematic landscape, for many, has become a gauntlet of graphic content. Profanity laces dialogue with increasing frequency. Scenes of blood and gore are not merely incidental; they are often the central focus, meticulously crafted to shock and disturb. I'm not suggesting that all films adhere to this aesthetic, but a significant portion of mainstream entertainment seems to revel in pushing the boundaries of what was once considered taboo. The concern, as voiced in our Sunday school class, is the cumulative effect of this constant exposure, particularly on young minds who may come to perceive such extreme depictions as commonplace, even normal.

Adding another layer of complexity to this media saturation is the growing trend toward what some perceive as an overzealous pursuit of political correctness. It seems that certain narratives and themes are being amplified, sometimes at the expense of traditional values or broader appeal, ostensibly to ensure representation and appease specific interest groups. While the intention behind inclusivity may be laudable, the execution often feels forced, even alienating to those who don't necessarily align with these particular viewpoints. I won't delve into naming specific groups, as the undercurrent of my concern is likely clear.

This brings me to a personal struggle. While I strive to adhere to Jesus's teaching of hating the sin but loving the sinner, I confess that I often find myself weary of what feels like a constant and often unapologetic flaunting of lifestyles that diverge from my own deeply held beliefs. As a straight, white, Christian male, I don't feel the need to broadcast my identity to every passerby. It simply feels like a personal conviction, a foundation upon which I build my life. Yet, the prevailing cultural wind often seems to favor the outspoken and the demonstrative, sometimes creating a sense that traditional values are being marginalized or even ridiculed.

It strikes me that somewhere along the line, the fundamental understanding of right and wrong has become increasingly blurred, even inverted. What was once widely considered morally reprehensible is now often presented as acceptable, even celebrated, while traditional values are increasingly labeled as outdated or intolerant. It's no wonder, then, that young people navigating this shifting terrain might look at the intense violence and the challenging social norms presented in the media and simply shrug, their sense of shock dulled by constant exposure and a perceived lack of clear moral anchors.

It's a far cry from the generation that stormed the beaches of Normandy, a generation united in a clear and unwavering fight against tyranny, a generation that understood the profound difference between right and wrong and was willing to sacrifice everything to defend the principles of freedom. Today's generation, facing a bewildering array of fluid identities and shifting social norms, often seems to lack that same sense of shared moral clarity.

The Allure of the Abyss: Why Disturbing Content Persists

Returning to the initial point about desensitization, I've never quite grasped the appeal of the horror genre. Even in its earlier iterations, while perhaps more reliant on suspense and suggestion, it held little attraction for me. But the horror films of today often dispense entirely with subtlety. They seem driven by a relentless pursuit of visceral shock, a competition to depict the most gruesome acts of torture and violence with maximum blood, guts, and gore. The creativity seems to lie not in building suspense or exploring psychological terror, but in devising ever more elaborate and disturbing ways to inflict suffering on screen.

I've heard accounts of people walking out of such movies in disgust, succumbing to nausea, even fainting or requiring medical attention due to the sheer level of disturbing content. It begs the question: what is the underlying appeal of such visceral negativity? While I may not fully comprehend it, I suspect that these kinds of movies and the hyper- violent video games that often accompany them are, in large part, targeted at a younger demographic. The more frequently these intense images are consumed, the more hardened individuals become to their impact, the more desensitized they are to violence and suffering. And I can't help but feel that this desensitization is precisely where "the evil one" wants them, in a state of emotional detachment and moral ambiguity.

This pervasive darkness in our media landscape underscores the critical need for God's protection in our lives, now more than ever. We are surrounded by forces that seek to drag us down, to erode our moral compass, and to normalize the very things that stand in opposition to His light. Therefore, the counsel remains as vital as ever: stay rooted in the Word of God, our ultimate source of truth and guidance, and heed the apostle Paul's timeless wisdom to "pray about everything, and worry about nothing." In a world increasingly saturated with darkness, our connection to the divine is our most powerful shield.

Chapter 10:
The Serenity of the Cast:
Finding God in the Great Outdoors

My lifelong passion, the hobby that truly calms my spirit and brings me immense joy, is fishing. My earliest memory of it takes me back to my childhood, a day spent with my papa. He took me to the water for the very first time, rod in hand, ready to introduce me to what would become a lifelong pursuit. Yet, I didn't get "hooked" (no pun intended) on it then. As a young boy, patience was a virtue that simply wasn't mine. I remember my restless energy getting the better of me, and soon, rocks, sticks, and anything else I could find would be sailing into the water. Needless to say, I got into quite a bit of trouble for those aquatic disruptions!

My papa, however, possessed the patience of a true angler, perhaps even the patience of a solid rock. Whether the sun was scorching or the cold was biting, if he intended to go fishing, he was there, steadfast and unwavering. As I grew older, my own appreciation for fishing deepened. It gradually transformed from a mere pastime into my ultimate escape, my way to detach from the hustle and bustle of everyday life. There's nothing quite like being out on a tranquil lake or a meandering river, with nothing on your mind but the quiet contemplation of the fish below and the immense pleasure of simply enjoying God's magnificent creation. People often ask me if I've ever tried fly fishing, and my answer is always a firm no. For many, it's a relaxing pursuit, but for me, it feels like too much work, too much intricate manipulation. My kind of fishing is about simplicity, about letting go and soaking in the natural world.

Returning to the idea of God's creation, it truly baffles me how anyone can immerse themselves in nature – whether it's fishing, camping, hiking, or simply taking a leisurely walk – gaze upon the breathtaking beauty and intricate design of all that God has made, and then declare it all to be some grand cosmic accident. The notion that everything began with a colossal explosion, and that all life somehow spontaneously emerged from primeval slime over millions of years, seems profoundly illogical when faced with the undeniable evidence of intelligent design all around us. As it so clearly states in Genesis, "In the beginning, God created the heavens and the earth." And what a job He did!

My advice, regardless of your personal interests, whether it's fishing or anything else that draws you outdoors, is this: get out there and actively enjoy God's creation. It's not just a pleasant diversion; it's genuinely good for your soul. It offers perspective, peace, and a profound connection to the divine artist who crafted it all.

Chapter 11:
The Everyday Divine:
Recognizing God's Little Miracles

I've been contemplating the countless small miracles God has bestowed upon us, the ones we often overlook in the rush of daily life. The thought began quite simply, as I was looking at my own hand, specifically my thumb. It struck me then, with an almost profound clarity: my thumb itself is an undeniable miracle. Have you ever attempted even the simplest of tasks without the full, opposing grasp of your thumbs? Imagine trying to tie your shoelaces, those mundane loops and knots becoming an insurmountable challenge. Or consider the intricate dexterity required to button a shirt, the tiny disc slipping through its precise slit, or the smooth glide of a zipper. Even picking up a simple cup of coffee or firmly grasping a tool becomes a nearly impossible feat. The thumb, this seemingly ordinary appendage, is the key to so much of our interaction with the physical world, a testament to intelligent design that allows us to manipulate, create, and connect. Its intricate musculature, unique position, and remarkable range of motion are functions we perform countless times a day without a second thought, yet without it, our world would crumble into a series of frustrating impossibilities.

And what about our eyes and ears? All of our senses, really, are equally miraculous. Where would we truly be without the gift of sight, to witness the vibrant hues of a sunset or the intricate details of a loved one's face? What would life be like without the symphony of sound – the laughter of children, the gentle patter of rain, the melody of a favorite song? Each sense is a complex, finely tuned instrument, interpreting the world around us and allowing us to experience its richness. I hold immense, unreserved respect for those who have navigated life having lost one or more of these precious senses, or perhaps never possessing them at all. Their ability to adapt, to perceive the world through different means, to find joy and purpose despite profound challenges, is truly awe-inspiring. Those individuals, more than anyone, truly understand the profound and often-unacknowledged gift they once possessed, or the unique ways their remaining senses compensate. Indeed, our entire body, from the smallest cell to the most complex organ system, is a testament to God's miraculous craftsmanship. It is the very miracle of life itself, self-regulating, repairing, and adapting in ways that science continues to uncover with wonder.

Now, let me be clear: I do not subscribe to the belief that life spontaneously crawled out of some primordial soup millions of years ago, or that the astonishing complexity of our universe and the life within it are merely the result of a "big explosion." Life does not originate from nothingness; order does not emerge from chaos without an ordering force. My conviction is that God is the creator of all things, the ultimate architect of this intricate and wondrous existence we inhabit. I believe, with a deepening certainty, that we often overlook these countless small miracles, these everyday blessings that define our very existence. We frequently fail to pause and truly appreciate what it would be like if a limb were suddenly taken away, a sense was lost, or a vital organ ceased to function. I honestly cannot fully imagine the profound challenges that those who have experienced such loss face each day, and as I've said before, I have nothing but unwavering admiration for their incredible strength, tenacity, and determination in adapting and striving to live a life that is as normal and fulfilling as possible. Their resilience serves as a powerful reminder of the preciousness of every functioning part of our being.

I write this now, perhaps, because I feel my own body beginning to betray me in small, insidious ways. First, there's the ongoing autoimmune issue affecting my back, a persistent ache that often dictates the limits of my day. Then, my one "good" knee is trying to compensate for the strain on my back, bearing an unfair burden, and now, my hips are beginning to protest, doing the same dance of compensation. I could list my growing catalogue of ailments at length, each one a minor rebellion against the smooth functioning I once took for granted, but I won't bore you with the intricate details of my troubles. I will, however, acknowledge one undeniable and universal truth: age. It inevitably catches up to all of us, a relentless tide that gradually erodes the youthful vigor we once commanded. I recall a vivid moment from long ago, when I was still working, a younger man perhaps too quick to complain. I was serving a sweet, older lady, meticulously counting out her change at the register. I clumsily dropped a coin on the floor. As I bent over to retrieve it, the effort drew an involuntary groan from me as I straightened back up. "Boy, I'm getting old," I remarked, more to myself than to her. She looked back at me, her eyes twinkling with a wisdom born of experience, and said, with a gentle firmness, "You can't be a wuss and get old." Her words, delivered with such quiet authority, have stayed with me ever since; she was absolutely, profoundly right. It was a simple statement, yet it encapsulated a lifetime of resilience, a reminder that aging demands not just physical endurance, but a certain mental fortitude and grace.

So, I suppose the underlying reason I'm writing this, these reflections on the body and its slow decay, is to urge you, and myself, with heartfelt sincerity, not to take God's small, everyday miracles for granted. These precious gifts—our sight, our hearing, the nimble dexterity of our hands, the very breath in our lungs— can be taken away at any time, often without warning. We frequently don't fully value them, truly appreciate their indispensable role in our lives, until we face the stark prospect of their loss. It's a call to conscious gratitude, a reminder to acknowledge the divine hand in the ordinary.

Finally, beyond all the physical blessings and their temporal nature, I want to emphasize the most profound loss of all, a tragedy far greater than any physical ailment or lost sense:

to die without knowing Jesus. If you don't know Him, if you haven't yet invited Him into your life, I encourage you, with all sincerity, to simply ask. It truly is that simple. There's no complex ritual, no elaborate confession, no long list of requirements. Just a genuine, open heart, willing to receive. Consider the transformative possibility, the profound shift in perspective, purpose, and eternal destiny that such a simple request can bring. He can, and will, change your life in ways you cannot yet imagine, filling voids that no earthly miracle, no amount of material possession, can ever truly satisfy.

Chapter 12:
The Fiery Within: Wrestling with the Grip of Anger

This one is a tough chapter for me to write about, a deeply personal and somewhat uncomfortable introspection. I've been thinking about it a lot recently, and I genuinely feel a sense of regret about my struggles with a quick temper. It's a part of myself I've long battled. I get frustrated very easily, and when that threshold is crossed, the reaction can be intense. Most of the time, this anger manifests as a destructive force directed at inanimate objects, leading me to inadvertently break things I happen to be working on. The sheer amount of money I've wasted, the countless hours spent repairing or replacing items due to my temper, weighs on me. If only I could recoup all the costs incurred by losing my composure and breaking things, I'd likely have a substantial sum. One thing I typically don't do, however, unless I become truly enraged with someone, is confront them face-to-face.

I'm quite shy in that regard. It's difficult for me to initiate a direct conversation to resolve conflict. I know I should be better at that, at articulating my feelings constructively rather than letting them fester or explode in other ways.

My frustration also frequently surfaces when I'm driving. Yes, I admit to experiencing road rage. Please don't misunderstand; I would never intentionally harm anyone, nor would I ever let my anger escalate to physical violence. However, the things I say, and sometimes even shout, while behind the wheel are certainly not good, and definitely not reflective of the person I aspire to be. Beyond those explosive moments, I also have a tendency to hold grudges. Sometimes these resentments can linger for years, a heavy burden I carry unnecessarily. This, too, is unhealthy. I can recall specific incidents from my childhood that I still struggle to let go of, minor slights or perceived injustices that have clung to my memory long past their relevance. Keeping such feelings held in for extended periods is simply detrimental to one's peace of mind and spiritual well-being. It creates an internal pressure cooker, waiting for the smallest spark to ignite.

As I've grown older, I believe I've made progress in controlling my temper. The outbursts are less frequent, and I can often recognize the warning signs before they fully erupt. Yet, there are undeniably still times when that familiar anger surges forth, catching me off guard. The Bible offers profound wisdom on this very struggle. In Ephesians 4:26, it says, "If you become angry, do not let your anger lead you to sin, and do not stay angry all day." This verse serves as a powerful reminder that while anger itself might be a natural human emotion, it's how we respond to it that matters. Giving in to uncontrolled anger, allowing it to dictate our actions, simply gives the devil a foothold in our lives. We must not give him that opportunity, because he is ever vigilant and will certainly take advantage of any opening we provide. He thrives on discord, resentment, and the chaos that uncontrolled anger breeds.

When I feel those familiar feelings of frustration and anger begin to surface, I try to seize the opportunity immediately to turn to God. I make a conscious effort to talk to Him, asking Him to gently take those feelings of anger away and to calm my spirit. Having a direct conversation with God, laying bare my struggles and vulnerabilities before Him, is the absolute best way to find relief, whether the burden is big or small, fleeting or deeply rooted. As Paul so eloquently states in Philippians 4:6, "Don't worry about anything, pray about everything." This timeless advice is a blueprint for managing all of life's anxieties and emotional turmoil, including anger. It teaches us to surrender our burdens and trust in a power far greater than our own.

I know, from personal experience, that trying to control your temper can be incredibly difficult at times. It demands immense self-awareness and discipline. However, for your own well-being—for your mental, emotional, and spiritual health—it's truly best to do the hard work of managing it. And, as I emphasized, prayer is the indispensable tool. You simply cannot do it alone. Trust me on this. I have tried to conquer this battle through sheer willpower and self-control, and it didn't come close to working. The devil is a strong adversary, cunning in his temptations, but God is infinitely stronger. His power is limitless, and His grace is sufficient for all our weaknesses.

Put your trust completely in God. He will never let you down. He is the unwavering anchor in the stormy seas of emotion, the source of peace that transcends all understanding, and the ultimate strength in every battle we face.

Chapter 13:
The Cosmos and the Unseen:
Beyond the Final Frontier

Space, the final frontier... these are the voyages... I digress, but yes, I'm a huge Star Trek fan. The allure of the cosmos, the vast, shimmering expanse beyond our atmosphere, has always captivated me. I love to stargaze, to simply lie back and look up into the endless tapestry of the night sky, a canvas ablaze with countless distant suns. And as I do, I inevitably wonder: if God, the Creator of all that is, fashioned anything else out there, specifically, other forms of life. Whether you identify as a Christian or not, the sheer scale of the universe naturally compels one to ponder the possibility of extraterrestrial beings, of "aliens" existing somewhere beyond our small blue planet.

The true, broad definition of an alien is simply "anything that belongs to a foreign territory." If we're discussing outer space, the definition narrows to "belonging to another planet." By that measure, anything from another world is, by its very nature, as alien as you can possibly get. However, when most people refer to "aliens," their minds conjure images of the popular cultural depiction: the stereotypical little grey men with oversized heads and huge, dark eyes. On that specific image, what does scripture have to say? Not much directly. The Bible doesn't offer detailed descriptions of beings from distant planets. Yet, it does speak extensively about spiritual beings – entities like angels and demons – that interact, often profoundly, within our human world. If one chooses to apply the term "alien" to these spiritual beings, then yes, in that sense, there are "aliens" in the Bible.

However, if we want to get technical and precise about it, angels and demons are fundamentally spiritual entities. They are not biological organisms existing on another physical planet, breathing oxygen or consuming food as we understand it. Their existence transcends the physical laws of our universe. We can be absolutely certain, based on scripture, that God created the entire universe, visible and invisible. And we know with equal certainty that Jesus Christ came specifically to save humanity, to redeem us from sin and reconcile us with God. The Bible, in its vast narrative from Genesis to Revelation, does not explicitly mention or detail life on other planets, nor does it present any need for salvation for non-human planetary inhabitants. Its focus is firmly on God's relationship with humankind on Earth.

So, is it possible for someone to have what is genuinely a spiritual encounter, perhaps a demonic experience, and mistakenly interpret it as having been in touch with an "alien" from outer space? Well, yes, it's entirely plausible. The Bible frequently talks about the reality of "fighting a spiritual enemy with weapons not of this world." These spiritual battles are not against flesh and blood, but against unseen forces, principalities, and powers of darkness. The enemy is deceptive, capable of masquerading as "an angel of light," and can certainly manipulate perceptions to create convincing illusions. As far as angels go, they too can certainly be mistaken for "aliens" or even for ordinary humans. They often appear in human form in biblical accounts, yet they don't seem to stay on Earth for extended periods of time, usually appearing to deliver a message or perform a specific task before departing. Hebrews 13:2 offers a pertinent reminder: "Do not forget to show hospitality to strangers, for by so doing some people have shown hospitality to angels without knowing it." This verse highlights the fact that angels can indeed walk among us, indistinguishable from ordinary people.

Therefore, in the grand scheme of theological understanding, and based on what scripture reveals, there are no "aliens" from other physical planets in the way popular culture often imagines them. Instead, the universe, as it relates to spiritual interaction with humanity, is populated by angels and demons. The clear message then is: watch out for the demons, for their intentions are malevolent and deceptive. And conversely, show genuine hospitality and kindness to strangers, for you never know—they just might be an angel, a messenger of God, crossing your path.

Live long and prosper.

Chapter 14:
The Shadow of the Serpent:
Navigating the Rising Tide of Evil

I'm not trying to be a downer here, or to dwell excessively on the darker aspects of our world, but a recent experience left a profound impression on me. I just watched the movie *The Sound of Freedom* for the first time. It's an exceptionally powerful film, but undeniably difficult to watch. If you've seen it, you'll understand the emotional weight it carries; if not, I truly believe it's a movie everyone needs to see to grasp the unsettling realities it portrays.

With that experience fresh in my mind, I found myself contemplating the pervasive nature of evil that seems to be engulfing the world today. It often feels as though Satan is having a field day, sowing discord and darkness across every facet of society. This insidious influence seems to extend from the very halls of government, where integrity and service are often overshadowed by self-interest and corruption, to the alarming increase in crime rates that plague our communities, eroding the sense of safety and order. Even our educational institutions, which should be bastions of truth and reason, seem to be shifting in their teachings, and the pervasive creep of "political correctness" appears to be influencing even our churches, muting essential truths for the sake of cultural acceptance. It truly seems that everything that was once considered morally right is now being inverted and labeled as wrong, and conversely, what was once unequivocally wrong is now being championed as right. This moral inversion is disorienting and deeply troubling.

Christians, who historically have been a bedrock of moral values in many societies, are increasingly finding themselves persecuted, marginalized, or openly mocked for their beliefs. Simultaneously, certain groups, driven by ideologies of hate and intolerance, are actively attempting to eradicate Israel and the Jewish people, and tragically, these cowardly groups often seem to operate with impunity, escaping accountability for their heinous actions. In our own country, there appears to be a disturbing application of two different standards of justice: one set of rules for the wealthy elite, the powerful, and those who align with certain political or social narratives, and an entirely different, harsher set of rules for the rest of us, the ordinary citizens. This blatant disparity undermines the very foundation of justice and fairness. The "woke" movement, too, has become increasingly tiresome and, frankly, illogical. The idea of biological men, who identify as women, competing in women's sports and using women's private spaces like locker rooms and restrooms, simply because they "think" they are women, dismisses biological reality and fairness to women. And "gay pride" is another example. Now, let me be clear: I genuinely do not care what someone chooses to do in the privacy of their own bedroom; that is their personal affair. My concern arises when these aspects of personal life are overtly paraded, glorified, and shoved into public view in ways that feel confrontational or demand universal affirmation. Jesus Himself provided the perfect model for navigating such complexities, saying to "love the sinner and hate the sin." That is precisely what I strive to do in my own life, extending grace to individuals while refusing to condone behaviors that stand in opposition to biblical truth.

Furthermore, I am profoundly tired of the incessant discourse surrounding racism. It feels as though this issue has become utterly out of hand, to the point where one can barely express an opinion without being immediately labeled a "racist," often without any genuine justification or understanding. This constant accusation is not only draining but utterly ridiculous; it's reached a point where I sometimes feel like giving up on it all and simply retreating into my own small, private world, shielded from the relentless cultural battles.

However, the reason I try to keep going, the unwavering hope that anchors me amidst this overwhelming tide of darkness, is that I know who ultimately wins in the end: Jesus. The Devil, despite his temporary successes and rampant activity, knows this too. He understands his ultimate defeat is assured. So, if you find yourself sick of it all, feeling utterly disheartened and just wanting to surrender, remember the timeless wisdom that Paul imparts in Philippians 4:6: "Don't worry about anything, but pray about everything with thanksgiving." Engaging with scripture regularly helps immensely; it provides perspective, comfort, and unwavering truth in a world that often feels devoid of it.

So remember, no matter who occupies the highest office, whether it be a president, a king, a dictator, or any other worldly ruler, their power is fleeting and finite. God is still the King. His sovereignty is absolute, His dominion eternal, and His ultimate victory is guaranteed.

This profound truth is the only enduring solace in the face of escalating evil.

Chapter 15:
The Paradox of Time:
Navigating the Seasons of Getting Older

I woke up this morning and, with a subtle shift in the air, I realized: I'm a year older. The day has been punctuated by a steady stream of birthday greetings, which I genuinely appreciate, each message a kind reminder that another year has etched itself onto the timeline of my life. Yet, amidst the well wishes, there's an undeniable, often bittersweet, truth that settles in: I am, indeed, getting older. It's a strange and unique position I find myself in, one where my outward appearance doesn't quite match the internal reality of my age. Many people comment that I don't look my age, but inwardly, man, do I feel it. Every creak, every ache, every slight diminishment in energy serves as a constant, quiet reminder of the years accumulating. And, perhaps paradoxically, I don't act my age ninety percent of the time either. I often feel as if I'm perpetually stuck between two distinct generations, caught in an odd chronological limbo. I'm too old, in some ways, for the genuinely young people, unable to fully relate to their world or their fresh perspectives. Yet, I act too young for the older people, often finding their slower pace or more settled routines don't quite align with my own still-restless spirit. The truth is, I'm not entirely sure where I truly belong in the grand tapestry of age groups.

Like I've said before, I generally just go my own way. This independent path has been my consistent mode of operation for most of my life, and through it all, God has graciously kept me here, guiding my steps even when they seemed meandering. I am, however, having considerable trouble with the concept of getting older, primarily because I simply don't know where all the time went. It feels as if large swaths of my life have evaporated, leaving behind only faint echoes. As I've reflected in another thought, the older you get, the faster time seems to accelerate, blurring the years into an indistinguishable rush. There are moments, often during quiet reflection, when I deeply wish I could go back in time, just for a brief conversation with my younger self. I'd impart some crucial advice, perhaps offer a glimpse of what to expect, and maybe, just maybe, armed with that foresight, things would have unfolded differently. The temptation to alter past decisions, to smooth out rough edges, or to simply reassure that younger version of myself, is a powerful one.

But, alas, such time travel remains purely in the realm of wistful thought. So, I guess I'll simply have to keep making the very best of things the way they are, accepting the present with its joys and challenges. The only constant, the only unwavering certainty, is to keep trusting God, because I firmly believe He does indeed have a plan, and His timing, though often inscrutable to our limited human understanding, is always perfect.

Thank you, Mom. I love you.

Chapter 16:
A Life Through Time:
Echoes of History and Personal Milestones

I suppose I can comfortably be classified as a baby boomer, a designation that carries with it the unique perspective of having lived through, and directly witnessed, a remarkable span of history. My lifetime has been marked by a staggering succession of pivotal events, each leaving its indelible mark on the collective consciousness and, more intimately, on my own memory. Here are some of those moments, as I recall them, woven into the fabric of my personal journey.

The farthest back I can reliably remember is the somber spectacle of John F. Kennedy's funeral. The only reason this particular event stands out so vividly in my young mind is because, for days, television networks across the nation took off all the beloved Saturday morning cartoons, replacing them with continuous, grayscale coverage of the procession and ceremonies. For a child, the absence of familiar animated heroes was a jarring indicator that something profoundly important, and deeply sad, was unfolding. Next, I suppose, came the escalating conflict in Vietnam. I, like many children of my generation, grew up with the omnipresent shadow of that war flickering across our television screens. It was a nightly ritual: the news would begin, and there, amidst the mundane reports, would be raw footage from the battlefields, often grim and unsettling. As a child, I never truly grasped the complex geopolitical intricacies, the shifting alliances, or the underlying reasons for the conflict; all I understood was that it was a war, a distant, brutal reality constantly intruding upon our living rooms.

Then came the seismic year of 1968. For a kid growing up in a small town, far removed from the cultural epicenters, it was truly a weird time. The concept of a "hippie" was utterly alien to me. "A hippie? What's a hippie?" I recall wondering, with genuine childish confusion, whether it might be some exotic animal from Africa. Growing up in a quiet, insulated small town, we simply didn't have hippies. My understanding of this burgeoning counterculture, like so much else of the outside world, had to be gleaned from the flickering images and limited narratives presented on television. When I finally saw these people – with their long hair, unconventional clothing, and radically different lifestyles – I remember thinking they were just plain strange, utterly unlike anyone I knew. And the rock and roll music that the hippies embraced, with its loud, often discordant sounds, seemed just as weird and unsettling as their appearance.

The seventies then arrived, bringing with them their own defining cultural and political touchstones. The undeniable centerpiece of that decade was the Watergate scandal. The simplified version, as I understood it then and recall it now, is that Republicans operating under President Nixon's administration broke into the Democrat headquarters located in the Watergate Hotel in Washington D.C. The scandal spiraled, leading to an unprecedented constitutional crisis and ultimately culminating in Nixon's resignation, a truly monumental event in American history. From that point on, any major scandal that erupts seems to inevitably be appended with the suffix "-gate," a lasting linguistic legacy of that tumultuous era. I graduated in the mid-seventies, and after that, nothing much of equivalent national or global impact stands out in my memory until the next decade rolled around.

Then the eighties hit, and hit they certainly did, with a vibrant, often excessive, force. The very beginning of that decade saw the exciting kick-off of my radio career, a personal milestone that would define a significant portion of my professional life. Ronald Reagan was in the White House, and the economy, for many, was booming. It was, as I've often heard it called, the "decade of decadence," and it truly lived up to that moniker. There seemed to be an abundance of money flowing, and with it, a culture of indulgence. It was, in many ways, an era of sex, drugs, and rock and roll – but not the folk-tinged, mellow sounds the hippies embraced. This was a different breed of rock: defined by spandex and leather, gravity-defying big hair, screaming guitar solos, and pounding, driving drumbeats.

They certainly don't make music like that anymore, or at least not with the same widespread cultural dominance. In retrospect, I think there was so much sheer fun, so much focus on outward enjoyment and material prosperity, that perhaps many of us paid insufficient attention to what was truly going on beneath the surface, the quieter, more serious shifts in the world.

Amidst the vibrant energy of the eighties, darker events unfolded. There was the assassination attempt on President Reagan, a chilling moment that brought the fragility of leadership into sharp focus. The decade also saw devastating acts of terrorism, such as the bombing of Pan Am Flight 103 over Lockerbie, Scotland, which tragically claimed the lives of 270 innocent people. Before that, the bombing of the American military barracks in Beirut, Lebanon, killed 220 Marines and 18 sailors, another horrific reminder of global instability. Both of these attacks were carried out by cowardly terrorist organizations, leaving indelible scars on our national consciousness. The nineties then came and went, a decade that, if you're reading this, you are probably old enough to remember quite clearly what transpired then. If not, a quick conversation with your parents will likely fill in the historical gaps.

The same general sentiment goes for the dawn of the new millennium. I vividly remember looking at my watch on New Year's Eve, 1999, anticipating the arrival of the new century with a mixture of excitement and a touch of the unknown. And while there were many defining moments in the early 2000s, I cannot bring this reflection to a close without specifically mentioning September 11th, 2001. I think that date, by itself, is enough said; its resonance and tragic significance are universally understood. On a lighter, more whimsical note, I did stay up until midnight on December 21st, 2012, to see what was supposedly going to happen when the Mayan calendar ended. The pervasive buzz suggested the world was going to end, or at least some really bad, cataclysmic event would unfold. After all the anticipation, I just went out and bought a new calendar for the following year.

Ultimately, there is only one being who truly knows when the world will end, and He, in His infinite wisdom, has not seen fit to reveal that specific timing to us. Well, there are probably countless other events and experiences that I've lived through, moments that have shaped me and the world around me, but there simply isn't enough time or space to recount them all here. More likely, the latter reason holds true: I just can't remember them all, as memory, like time itself, can be a fleeting and selective master.

Chapter 17:
Idols of the Modern Age: The Allure of False Gods

This contemplation takes me back to ancient times, as recounted in the Bible, when people routinely engaged in the worship of idols and individuals who audaciously claimed divine status. There were deities for every conceivable aspect of existence: the god of the sun, the god of fertility, the god of war, and countless others. Human hands meticulously carved images of these gods from wood, stone, or metal, erected them in temples and homes, and then bowed down in fervent worship. I confess, I've always struggled to truly grasp the human inclination to do that—to create and worship something tangible and limited, when the one true, living God, the very Creator of the universe, was, and is, so readily available to those who seek Him. The profound disconnect between the inherent power of the divine and the meager creations of human hands remains a puzzling aspect of human history.

Even today, in our seemingly advanced and sophisticated world, people continue to have their gods, though the forms they take are often far less overt than ancient statues. These modern idols are perhaps more insidious because they are often intangible, subtly weaving themselves into the fabric of our desires and aspirations. Consider, for instance, the fervent adoration showered upon professional athletes, whose incredible feats of physical prowess can elevate them to near-mythical status. Or the almost spiritual devotion directed towards music stars and movie celebrities, whose lives are followed with an intensity that borders on religious fervor. Then there's the relentless pursuit of material possessions, the yearning for "stuff" that none of one's friends possess, the desire for exclusivity and outward displays of wealth—a testament to the deceptive power of consumerism. And undoubtedly, the most pervasive and widely worshipped god in contemporary society, often without conscious acknowledgment, is money. While it's undeniably true that we all require money to live, to meet our basic needs and navigate the complexities of modern existence, that essential truth does not, and should not, mean we must elevate it above all other things, allowing it to dictate our priorities, our values, and our very sense of self-worth. Matthew 6:24 perfectly encapsulates this spiritual dichotomy, stating with absolute clarity: "No one can serve two masters, for he will hate the one and love the other, or he will be devoted to the one and despise the other. You cannot serve God and money." This verse serves as a timeless warning against divided loyalties, reminding us that our ultimate allegiance must rest with one master alone.

There is, fundamentally, only one living God and Creator, and He is the "Great I Am," the self-existent, eternal, and all-powerful being. All other gods, whether historical deities or modern-day idols, are either long dead, having never truly existed beyond human imagination, or are mere fleeting constructs of a fallen world. When I look at crucifixes, those poignant depictions of Christ's sacrifice, I often find myself thinking about the crosses I own, the ones that hang in my home or rest on my desk. On those crosses, Jesus is not still affixed, for He arose triumphantly from the dead. The empty cross is a powerful symbol of resurrection and victory, a profound distinction from the static, lifeless idols of other faiths. It signifies a living, active, and conquering God, not a defeated or confined one.

The first of the Ten Commandments, given directly by God, unequivocally states: "I am the Lord your God, who brought you out of the land of Egypt, out of the house of slavery. You shall have no other gods before me." This isn't merely a suggestion or a guideline; it is a divine commandment, a foundational principle for humanity's relationship with its Creator.

I suppose that, both in biblical times and in the present day, many individuals simply choose not to believe in the living God, or perhaps they have never truly encountered the profound truth of His existence. Ultimately, the full truth will be revealed on Judgment Day, when all will stand before their Creator. But in the interim, it is the sacred and imperative job of all Christians to spread the Good News, to share the word of God, and to tell people about our living Lord, Jesus Christ. We are called to plant the seed of faith, to share the truth of the Gospel. After that, it is the sacred and mysterious work of the Holy Spirit to cultivate that seed, to bring conviction, understanding, and transformation to hearts and minds. Jesus, and Jesus alone, is the only one who can truly save humanity from its fallen state and reconcile us to God.

John 3:16 captures this ultimate truth with unparalleled beauty and brevity: "For God so loved the world, that he gave his only Son, that whoever believes in him should not perish but have eternal life." It truly doesn't get any better or simpler than that. There are no elaborate ceremonies you have to undergo, no arduous pilgrimages to complete, no long lists of good deeds to accumulate in order to earn salvation. Nothing like that is required. Just like the thief on the cross, in his dying moments, simply asked for remembrance and received the promise of paradise, all you have to do is ask. It's that profoundly simple, yet unimaginably profound. The grace of God is freely given to all who believe.

Chapter 18:
A New Day Coming: The Power of Forgiveness

I fell out of bed the other morning – not a graceful descent, but a rather abrupt meeting with the floor. Still half asleep, I picked myself up, my senses lagging, and staggered into the kitchen. My stomach rumbled, signaling an undeniable hunger. I opened the refrigerator door, staring blankly for a moment at its contents before settling on a slice of cold pizza and a root beer. A truly gourmet breakfast, wouldn't you agree? I sat down at the table and began to eat, but as I chewed, my mind, perhaps fueled by the unconventional meal, began to wander.

I started to think about my life, a sweeping panorama of years and experiences. My memory drifted back to a pivotal moment: when I was saved up at summer camp. I must have been around six or seven years old at the time, and I recall it as a good, pure moment, a foundational experience in my spiritual journey. But then, my thoughts veered, as they often do, to all the things I had done since that time—the good, certainly, but also the bad, and regrettably, the downright ugly. It felt as though the bad and the ugly far outweighed the good, a heavy imbalance on the scales of my conscience. And that's when things really started to happen in my head, a swirling vortex of self-condemnation. For a moment, I genuinely thought I was going just a little bit crazy.

Amidst this internal turmoil, I heard a voice, sharp and accusatory, say, "Hey!" I looked around the empty kitchen, startled, and murmured, "What?" The voice immediately retorted, dripping with contempt, "You are such a fool." My confusion intensified. "What? Why?" I demanded. The voice pressed on, relentless: "You think after all the stupid things you have done in your life, God would want you? He won't let losers like you into heaven. Every day you're doing, or even thinking about, bad stuff that won't get you in. Think about that and see how you feel." And he was right. Every word resonated with my deepest fears and insecurities. As my grandfather used to say, I felt lower than a snake's belly in a wagon rut, utterly defeated and worthless.

Just about the time I had sunk to my absolute lowest, when the weight of my perceived failures seemed unbearable, the most calming voice I have ever heard spoke to me. It was gentle, yet undeniably powerful, cutting through the self-doubt and the harsh accusations. "Why are you listening to him?" the voice inquired, radiating peace. "Have you forgotten what I've taught you?" I confessed, a tremor in my voice, "Well, it has been a while." The truth was, I had let my focus drift, allowing the noise of my past mistakes to drown out the eternal truths.

The calming voice continued, tender yet firm: "There's your problem. You have been saved. You are a child of the King, and nothing or no one can ever take you away from Me." The words washed over me like a cleansing balm, an immediate antidote to the venom of the other voice. "Don't look back," it urged. "It has all been forgotten and forgiven. That dude over there, the one filling your head with doubt, he's the real loser, and he knows it. That's why he's trying to drag you down to his level, to make you feel as miserable and defeated as he is. Don't let him do it. Let Me say this one more time, with my blood you have been forgiven." The emphasis on "my blood" underscored the incredible sacrifice, the ultimate act of redemption that sealed my forgiveness.

Overwhelmed with gratitude and relief, I whispered, "I love and thank You." After what You did for me, what You sacrificed, the very least I can do is to live more like You, to emulate Your grace and love. With renewed resolve, I turned to the source of the condemning voice, the "real loser," and told him, with a newfound authority, to get lost. The profound moral of this experience, the core message that resonated deep within my soul, is clear: **Don't look back.** The past, with all its mistakes and regrets, is under the blood of Christ. There is always a new day coming, a fresh start, boundless grace. And, just as an amusing aside that broke the solemnity of the moment, after all that profound spiritual revelation, the calming voice added, "Cold pizza and root beer for breakfast? Really?" A touch of divine humor, a gentle reminder that even in our most serious moments, God is present, and sometimes, simply human.

Chapter 19:
The Priceless Gift: Understanding True Friendship

I know a lot of people, perhaps more than I can count, through various avenues of life— work, church, acquaintanceships that form and fade. Yet, despite this wide circle of connections, I have very few true friends. In fact, if I were to be honest, you could easily count the number of genuine friends I have on one hand. To me, a friend is someone who is consistently, reliably there for you, not just during moments of ease and celebration, but especially when life becomes challenging. A real friend is someone you can truly open up to, someone with whom you can share your deepest thoughts, fears, and joys without reservation or judgment. They are the person you can call at any hour, day or night, for help, knowing they will answer, ready to offer assistance, advice, or simply a listening ear. A real friend, by this definition, is an incredibly rare and precious commodity, hard to find in a world often characterized by superficial connections. And when you are fortunate enough to find such a person, you immediately recognize their value and never want to let them go.

I am blessed to have one such friend whom I have known since we were sophomores in high school. Our shared history stretches back decades, filled with countless memories, triumphs, and tribulations. Even though he now lives in Arizona, a considerable distance from me, we still make it a point to talk a couple of times a week. These conversations are vital, allowing us to keep each other informed about what's new in our lives, sharing both the mundane and the significant. Beyond him, I have a couple of wonderful friends within my church community. They are genuinely good people, individuals whose faith and character I deeply respect and admire. To me, a friend is someone who knows almost as much about you as your spouse, perhaps even more, discerning your unspoken thoughts and understanding your quirks and complexities. Or, in some profound instances, they might indeed know even more about you than your spouse, having been privy to different chapters or vulnerabilities. A true friend is someone you can often talk to with greater ease and unfiltered honesty than you might with your own family members, navigating difficult topics or personal struggles with a unique level of comfort and understanding.

The essence of this profound bond is beautifully articulated in the words of Jesus Himself. In John 15:12-13, He declares: "This is my commandment, that you love one another as I have loved you. Greater love has no one than this, that someone lay down his life for his friends." This isn't just a suggestion; it's a divine imperative, setting the ultimate standard for selfless affection and commitment. Jesus, our ultimate example, demonstrated this love by literally laying down His life for us, His friends. A real friend, one who embodies this kind of sacrificial love and unwavering loyalty, is an extraordinary blessing to have in your life. Therefore, when you are fortunate enough to discover such a person, someone who truly exemplifies what it means to be a friend, cherish that bond, hang onto that person with all your might, and do not let go. Such relationships are treasures beyond measure, reflecting a piece of divine love on Earth.

Chapter 20:
The Heart of the Season:
Restoring Christ to Christmas

Growing up, Christmas was, and unequivocally still is, my favorite time of the year. There's an undeniable magic to it, a pervasive spirit of joy and hope that seems to permeate the very air. Perhaps part of my enduring affection for the season stems from the fact that my birthday falls within the Christmas period, creating a double celebration. As a child, I absolutely loved everything about it: the thrill of waking up to presents under the tree, the warmth and laughter of family get-togethers, and simply the unique atmosphere of the season itself, steeped in carols and festive decorations. Oh, and let's not forget the much- anticipated Christmas vacation from school – a cherished break filled with freedom and fun. Now, my birthday isn't quite the momentous occasion it once was, a subtle reminder of the passage of time, but my deep love for the Christmas season remains as strong as ever.

When I was a kid, I certainly knew what Christmas was all about in a general sense, but I didn't truly grasp its profound meaning. My primary focus, as for many children, was undeniably the presents. There was one thing, however, that genuinely perplexed me, a question that lingered in my young mind: why did all the signs at the stores emblazon "Merry X-mas" instead of "Merry Christmas"? I always wondered about that mysterious 'X.' I asked everyone I knew, including my Sunday school teacher, trying to unravel the enigma of why 'X'? All of them, from well-meaning adults to those who should have known better, offered me the same explanation: it was merely a way to shorten the term, a convenient abbreviation because there simply wasn't enough room on the sign for the full word "Christmas."

Even then, that explanation always struck me as profoundly sad. It felt, even to a young mind, like they were symbolically "X-ing Christ out of Christmas," erasing the very essence of the celebration. And tragically, this practice persists to this day, even if you can find the term "Christmas" on public displays at all. Now, the politically correct term has largely become "Happy Holidays." This shift is often justified by the notion that someone, somewhere, might be offended by the explicit mention of Christmas. Yet, this approach misses the entire point. Christ is, unequivocally, the reason for the season. If it weren't for His miraculous birth, there would be no "Happy Holidays" to celebrate, no festive break, no widespread spirit of goodwill that permeates the end of the year. It is the birth of our Lord Jesus Christ that gives this time its foundational significance. Another aspect of the modern Christmas season that truly bothers me is its overwhelming commercialization.

The focus has tragically shifted from the spiritual significance of Christ's birth to the materialistic pursuit of profit. The prevailing question during this season seems to be, "How much money did stores make?" or "What are the latest sales figures?" It feels as though Christ has been systematically left out of almost everything that now constitutes Christmas. You can even face controversy or trouble for simply displaying a humble nativity scene in your own front yard, while a collection of reindeer and Santa Claus figures is perfectly acceptable and widely embraced. This selective permissiveness highlights a disturbing cultural disconnect.

What I am trying to convey, with a sense of urgency and deep conviction, is this: let's make a conscious effort to put Christ back in Christmas. Let's actively remember and celebrate the true reason for this blessed season. As a matter of fact, let's extend that principle beyond Christmas and strive to put Christ back into everything that we do, every single day. Imagine the profound transformation that would occur if we individually and collectively committed to living our lives in a way that honors Him. It would undoubtedly be better for every single person, for our communities, and for our nation as a whole. God Himself provides the blueprint for this transformation. He says in 2 Chronicles 7:14, "If my people, who are called by my name, will humble themselves and pray and seek my face and turn from their wicked ways, then I will hear from heaven, and I will forgive their sin and will heal their land." It really is that simple: seek His face, and He shall heal our land.

Remember this profound truth: It is not wrong to say "Merry Christmas." It is a joyous declaration of faith, a celebration of the greatest gift humanity has ever received.

Chapter 21:
The Shifting Sands of Time:
Reflections on Youth, Regret, and Divine Purpose

What exactly happened to time? It's a question that often echoes in my mind, a subtle yet persistent bewilderment. I vividly remember my childhood days in school, seated at my desk, my gaze perpetually fixed on the clock, its hands moving with what felt like excruciating slowness. Each minute crawled by as I waited, with breathless anticipation, for the bell signaling recess, then lunch, and finally, the cherished moment when it was time to go home. The journey to each of these milestones seemed to stretch into an eternity. And then, once home, the cycle quickly resumed. By the time homework was completed, chores were done, and all the day's obligations were met, it felt like mere moments before it was time for bed, only to wake and begin the school day all over again. The days, though seemingly endless in the moment, blurred into weeks, and weeks into months, without much conscious thought about their passage.

Now that I'm older, the concept of time has utterly transformed. It races by with such bewildering speed that I often have no clue where the years have gone. It feels as though there's still a kid inside me, perpetually wondering what on earth happened, how did we get here so fast? The stark reality is that while my body is undeniably getting older, and the physical reminders are increasingly frequent, I absolutely refuse to fully "grow up" in the traditional sense. I hold onto a certain youthful spirit, a reluctance to conform entirely to the expectations of aging. This often leaves me in a peculiar limbo, feeling too old for the truly young generations who inhabit a vastly different world, yet acting too young for my actual peers, whose lives may have settled into a more sedate rhythm.

With that being said, when I do allow myself to look back on my life, a profound sense of wonder often accompanies the review. I find myself pondering the "what ifs": what would have happened if I had made a different decision at a critical juncture, if I had chosen a path diverging from the one I actually took? I will, of course, never know the answers to these hypothetical questions, but the curiosity persists. I often wonder, for instance, what would have transpired if I had chosen *not* to accept that first radio job I was offered. That particular decision, in hindsight, marked the beginning of what I now refer to as my "heathen years"—a period during which I delved heavily into, well, let's just say a lifestyle deeply immersed in sex, drugs, and rock and roll. If I had chosen a different road, perhaps those less-than-ideal experiences would not have happened. Yet, conversely, I also would not have learned the profound lessons God was undoubtedly teaching me through those very experiences, lessons that have shaped me into the person I am today. I often reflect that I should have joined the service, a path that many of my peers took. However, at the

time I graduated, the Vietnam War was just winding down, and the very idea of it was genuinely scary to me. Plus, as a small side note, my nearsightedness was so severe back then that they likely wouldn't have accepted me anyway. I want to take a moment to express my profound respect and heartfelt thanks for all those who did serve; their sacrifice is immeasurable. There were a couple of times during those wilder years when I did things that, by all accounts, should have ended my life, but in His infinite mercy,

God pulled me out of those perilous situations and allowed me to live on. I believe firmly that He has a plan for me, though I don't know what it is yet. Perhaps, just perhaps, it is to write this very book, to share my story, and to tell people what God has done for me, demonstrating His enduring grace and transformative power.

God is undeniably good. He has shown me an incredible, long-suffering patience that I, in my humanity and my past mistakes, absolutely do not deserve. This boundless patience, this unwavering steadfastness in His relationship with me, tells me, more eloquently than words, that He loves me unconditionally. It assures me that all those bad things I did, all those regrettable choices, have been forgotten and forgiven through His grace. If you would like to know Jesus, to experience His love and forgiveness in the same profound way that I do, the path is incredibly simple. All you have to do is ask Him to save you, to come into your heart and transform your life. It really is that easy.

Chapter 22:
Serving Two Masters: The Choice for Eternity

I am, and have been since my high school days, a dedicated fan of rock music. When I was a younger man, my personal anthem might well have been "The louder the better." The raw energy, the sheer volume, it all resonated with a youthful exuberance. These days, I still listen to it, finding comfort and enjoyment in its familiar rhythms, but certainly not at the ear-splitting decibels of my youth. My ears, it seems, have accumulated their own wisdom over the years and simply can't handle that kind of sonic assault anymore.

Anyway, while listening to some music recently, I heard a song by Van Halen titled "The Best of Both Worlds." The phrase immediately got me thinking. It made me ponder how many people, consciously or unconsciously, are trying to achieve precisely that—the "best of both worlds." And more specifically, I began to consider how many Christians are attempting this very thing, striving to straddle the line between their faith and the allure of the secular world.

It seems to me that many churches these days—certainly not all, but a significant number—are inadvertently preaching a message that life as a Christian is nothing but unicorns, rainbows, and cotton candy. They present a version of faith that suggests unwavering ease, constant happiness, and a lack of real struggle or sacrifice. This portrayal is fundamentally misleading and, frankly, not right. It contradicts the very clear teachings of Jesus. In Luke 16:13, Jesus unequivocally states, "No servant can serve two masters, for either he will hate the one and love the other, or he will be devoted to the one and despise the other. You cannot serve God and money." I deeply believe that Jesus does not favor those who try to make it through life perpetually "sitting on the fence," refusing to commit fully to one side or the other. That's precisely why God, in His infinite wisdom, gave humanity the gift of choice. He compels us to make a decision, to get squarely on one side or the other, to commit our allegiance wholeheartedly. There is no middle ground in matters of ultimate devotion.

Jesus's words in that same verse powerfully underscore the unavoidable dichotomy: "you will hate one and love the other." God, the Creator of the universe, the giver of all life and breath, truly wants and absolutely deserves all of our praise, all of our glory, and our complete devotion. Consider the unimaginable sacrifice: Jesus, the Son of God, was brutally tortured and endured a violent, humiliating death on the cross. He suffered this agonizing fate not because He deserved it, but precisely because He loved us, a truth beautifully encapsulated in John 3:16: "For God so loved the world, that he gave his only Son, that whoever believes in him should not perish but have eternal life." Now, honestly ask yourself: has money, or any other material possession, any worldly ambition, or any transient pleasure ever done anything remotely comparable for you? Has any of the "stuff" of the world offered such a profound, life-altering, eternal sacrifice? If you choose to pursue the way of the world, prioritizing its fleeting pleasures and deceptive promises over God, then that is, ultimately, your choice. However, the Bible is clear and unwavering in its teaching: hell is a real place, a place of eternal separation from God, and it is a truly horrible place to spend eternity.

The bottom line is stark in its simplicity, yet profound in its implications: the choice is yours. As for me, I have made my decision. I am spending my eternity with Jesus in Heaven.

By the way, Heaven is also a real place, a glorious destination promised to those who believe. If you, too, desire to spend eternity there, to know Jesus in the same deeply personal and transformative way that I do, all you have to do is ask. That's it. Just ask. It's truly that simple, requiring no complex rituals, no elaborate ceremonies, no arduous works.

Remember the thief on the cross, who, in his dying moments, simply turned to Jesus and asked for remembrance. And Jesus's immediate, gracious response was, "Truly, I say to you, today you will be with me in Paradise." It's that simple, yet the implications are eternal.

Chapter 23:
Pondering the Peculiar:
A Collection of Curious Questions

Just some food for thought, a collection of intriguing questions to ponder, perhaps to wrap things up with a bit of whimsical contemplation. These are the kinds of queries that pop into the mind when one truly pauses to observe the quirks and paradoxes of our language, our customs, and the world around us. They are not meant to be profound philosophical statements, but rather amusing invitations to think a little differently about the everyday.

Let's begin with some sartorial confusion: If you possess only one shirt, why then do you typically own a "pair" of pants? Does a singular garment somehow imply a duality in its lower counterpart? It's a linguistic oddity that makes one wonder about the origins of such common phrases.

And in the realm of professions: Why do highly trained medical professionals, who dedicate years to mastering their craft, "have a practice"? Shouldn't they, by definition, be past the stage of practicing and instead be consummate masters of their field? It implies a continuous state of learning, even for those at the pinnacle of their expertise.

Our own bodies offer up some peculiar paradoxes: Why do noses run, often at the most inconvenient times, while feet, those trusty weight-bearers, seem to smell? The anatomical functions seem comically inverted in our everyday descriptors.

Then there's the hero of Metropolis: If bullets are famously depicted bouncing harmlessly off Superman, rendering him impervious to conventional gunfire, why did he always instinctively duck or flinch when someone merely threw a gun at him? It suggests a lingering, almost subconscious, vulnerability to the object itself, rather than its projectile.

Consider the precision of timekeeping: Why is the third hand on a clock, the one that sweeps around most rapidly, called the "second hand"? It dictates the seconds, yet its numerical position in the sequence of hands is clearly third.

And in the realm of personal growth: How can there truly be "self-help groups"? The very concept of a group implies external assistance, a collective effort, which seems to contradict the notion of singular "self-help." Is it self-help *within* a group, or merely a group that facilitates self-help?

Our culinary world isn't immune to these playful questions: Why does round pizza, a perfect circle, so often come packaged in a square box? The geometry seems a bizarre mismatch, an inefficiency of design that has simply been accepted as the norm. And what exactly did "cured" ham actually have that needed to be remedied or treated? Was it once ill? The term implies a healing process for a meat product.

Even the natural world has its whimsical queries: Do light winds, those gentle breezes, possess half the calories of their more robust, "regular" counterparts? A comical thought, as if air currents could be subject to dietary restrictions.

A question about accessibility: Why are there Braille dots on drive-up ATMs? The very nature of a drive-up machine implies the user is likely in a vehicle, making the tactile reading of Braille impractical, if not impossible, for most users.

And a classic thought experiment for the scientifically inclined: If you were somehow able to drive your vehicle at the literal speed of light, what then would happen when you turned your headlights on? Would the light even emanate, or would it simply become static relative to your vehicle?

Geographical anomalies provide further fodder: Why are there "interstate" highways in Hawaii, a state composed of islands, separated by vast stretches of ocean? The term "interstate" implies connection *between* states on a landmass.

Our very language for structures holds an amusing inconsistency: Why do we call them "apartments" when they are all stuck together, sharing walls and floors? And conversely, why do we refer to completed structures as "buildings" when, logically, they have already been "built"? Shouldn't they be called "builts" once construction is finished?

And a darkly humorous one: What exactly happens to a person when they get scared "half to death" twice? Does one cease to exist entirely, or is there some fraction of life remaining?

A question for the ages, especially for those who appreciate toast: What truly was the "best thing" before sliced bread, a seemingly indispensable convenience of modern life? The answer implies a time when bread, though perhaps delicious, was inconveniently whole.

And a common frustration for many: Why do banks impose an "insufficient funds" charge when you clearly don't have any money in the first place? It feels like a punitive measure that exacerbates the very problem it identifies.

Finally, a truly meta-linguistic challenge: If a word in the dictionary, the very arbiter of correct spelling, were itself misspelled, how would you, the reader, ever know? The source of truth would contain a hidden untruth.

There you go. A collection of peculiar questions, simple yet thought-provoking, designed to offer a bit of lighthearted contemplation and, perhaps, to remind us that even in the mundane, there are always intriguing details to consider. Stuff to think about indeed.

About the Author

This collection of thoughts marks my inaugural journey into the profound and often surprising world of writing, a venture I sincerely hope resonates deeply and personally with each reader who takes the time to turn its pages. Now standing at 67 years young, I've enthusiastically embarked on a new, more reflective chapter of life, having recently embraced retirement from a fulfilling and extensive career within the paint business. This particular professional endeavor followed a vibrant, indeed dynamic, two-decade period where I found immense satisfaction and engagement, immersing myself in the exciting and ever-evolving realm of radio, proudly serving as a DJ across various stations and truly connecting with listeners. My foundational academic pursuit, one that continues to inform and enrich my worldview, was deeply rooted in the study of history, a subject that has always held a profound and captivating fascination for me, consistently shaping my perspective on the intricate tapestry of the world around us.

The very genesis of this book was entirely organic, wonderfully unexpected, and quite humbling. It beautifully blossomed from what began as a simple, yet ultimately significant, act: sharing a few personal reflections and observations during a quiet Sunday service at my local church. The immediate and truly overwhelming encouragement I received from several members of the congregation proved to be the pivotal spark I needed, igniting a newfound sense of purpose. Their collective belief, expressed with such warmth and sincerity, that I should continue to explore, articulate, and share these burgeoning thoughts fueled a nascent idea within me. This burgeoning concept, through persistent effort, dedicated contemplation, and a genuine, heartfelt desire to share a piece of my journey, gradually coalesced and eventually took the tangible, satisfying shape of this very book. As I've openly mentioned, this entire endeavor represents my very first foray into the expansive and sometimes daunting landscape of authorship. It has been an unexpectedly deeply fulfilling, enriching, and profoundly revealing experience. My earnest and heartfelt hope is that you, the cherished reader, discover as much enjoyment, quiet introspection, meaningful connection, and perhaps even a touch of shared understanding within these pages as I did throughout the entire, unfolding process of bringing them thoughtfully and prayerfully to life.